I0441292

--- Libertarian History ---

LIBERTARIAN HISTORY

by LIN XUN

Dead Writers Club

--- Libertarian History ---

Copyright © 2016

Lin Xun & Dr. Rex Curry, Esq.,

All rights reserved.

ISBN-13:978-1535443265

ISBN-10:153544326X

THE DEAD WRITERS CLUB ALSO AUTHORED:

Drug Detection Dog Training

Lies My Teacher Told Me

Police State U.S.A.

Liberal Fascism

Prison Planet

COMING SOON

I Got Something You Can Pledge To Right Here!

America's Dumbest Criminals

When Ginger Put Her Hand Over Her Heart

--- **Libertarian History** ---

CONTENTS

	Table of Contents	5
	Dedication	9
	Forward by Kim Jong-un	10
1	History Against Liberty	14
2	Francis Bellamy: Ugly Friend	25
3	Edward Bellamy: Bellicose Militarist	42
4	Pledge of Allegiance Drills	49
5	The Civil War & Military Socialism	52
6	History of Masons	58
7	America goes to Germany	67
8	Swastikas = "S" shapes (SS, VW)	70
9	Holocausts & Wholecausts	85
10	Hitler's Socialist Mein Kampf	117

11	Signs & Signatures of Socialism	128
12	American Socialism in Italy	137
13	USA's August Landmesser	145
14	Yesteryears's Indoctrination	147
15	Background for this Book	154
16	Fight the Past & Present	161
17	Un-earthing Police Dog Fraud	166
18	Narcotics Dog Training	175
19	History of Drug Dogs	180
20	Police Dog Research	183
21	Lock Your Doors	187
22	Past & Future Police State	191
23	Guns & History	195
24	Not See Nazi Socialism	201
25	Training Dogs & Lizards	204

--- Libertarian History ---

26	Dog Economics 101	207
27	History of Socialist Programs	208
28	Water's Socialist Past	211
29	Woodman Spare that Old $10 Tree	215
30	Tree Laws Make Trees History	223
31	History of Government Schools	226
32	Triangle Shirtwaist Factory Fire	229
33	Dr. Karry's Amazing Discovery	233
34	The Crucifix	237
35	She Was Temperamental	238
36	Old Soviet Socialist Poetry	240
37	Capitalist Pearls	241
38	Democracy = Dumbocracy	242
	About the Author	243

--- **Libertarian History** ---

DEDICATION

The cliche' "History is written by the victors" is more accurately written "History is written by government schools (socialist schools)." The "history" that constitutes a student's brainwashing depends on where he attends G-schools (government schools).

The libertarian philosopher Harry Browne said that the biggest mistake ever made was letting the government educate children.

This book is dedicated to all victims of government (socialist) schools. This dedication includes those victims in the past, and those tomorrow morning and each morning thereafter.

Anarchists say: "The history that students in G-schools are NOT taught would fill a book." Or multiple books.

Here is one volume.

FORWARD
By Kim Jong-un

When Micky Barnetti at "No Pledge Publishing" first approached me about penning the forward to Lin Xun's book, I was honored. Barnetti delivered some galleys to me to review. After perusing them, I became infuriated. I invited Barnetti and Lin to chat with me at Camp 13 here in North Korea in order to clarify the many errors. They rudely declined my offer of gracious hospitality.

Lin's anti-socialist rant is absurd, and most Americans share every North Korean's love for socialism. We Koreans learned so much from the country where children chant the Pledge of Allegiance each day in government schools (socialist schools) as promulgated by the great American socialist Francis Bellamy, an inspiration to comrades worldwide.

Lin considers me to be the intellectual heir of Stalin, Mao, and Hitler. I surpass all of them combined. Besides, I am alive and at the peak of a socialist superman's strength. The average life expectancy in our utopia is eleven glorious years, and here I am at 160.

Lin's book is banned here in North Korea and that ban is redundant anyhoo in that her book will not be printed on our glorious people's printing presses. I hope your government will respect our laws and ban her book too and refuse to print it on your glorious people's presses.

I have instructed your media to withhold Lin's revelations about Dr. Rex Curry's historical discoveries. The media agreed and indicated that they have a long-standing practice of suppressing those facts and their silence will continue.

North Korea already has the greatest books, ebooks, computers, music, art, cinema, opera, architecture, radio stations, television, tourist resorts, "camping," bars, restaurants, shopping malls, toilet paper, deodorant, cars, motorcycles, yachts, shoes, shelter, clothing, food, dogs, cats, and everything. Our greatness was explained by my late father Kim Jong-il in his many books, all best-sellers here and available as e-books at the DPRK website for "free" download (for which you will be placed on the NSA watchlist and no longer allowed to fly). Our special e-books will liberate all personal information, photographs, contacts, and more that are on your computers and smartphones and share it with Pyongyang.

North Korea has the greatest history in the history of history. The reverse of this is not true.

At this time, I hereby order you to close this book right now and never open it again. Follow our political ideology of Juche (self-reliance) and boil your closed book to render a gruel nutritious enough for you to endure one more day of glorious socialist life. As the centerpiece of our universal free health care, your home-made book porridge can cure the deadly capitalist disease of obesity (it has cured the disease here).

Perhaps it is better that you die. You have not closed the book.

Micky Barnetti will die. We have the number that your police state uses to track and control everyone (the Social Security number, a.k.a. Socialist Slave number). Wherever Barnetti obtains a job or uses a credit card or bank, we will arrive with glorious socialist death.

Lin will die too, but we can't figure out if she has a slave number or where she is from (any comrade who knows please alert me).

Workers of the world unite!

your dear leader,

Kim Jong-un
Worker's Party of Korea
Pyongyang, Korea

--- **Libertarian History** ---

1. HISTORY AGAINST LIBERTY

What is "Libertarian History"? There are many hidden history lessons that most people never learn. The government's schools do not teach libertarian history.

What are the history lessons in the government's schools (socialist schools)? A popular maxim states: "Those who don't know history are doomed to repeat it." Socialist schools are DESIGNED to perpetuate ignorance in order to repeat the same errors.

Why does the "land of the free and the home of the brave" have schools operated by the government? How did the USA impose that emblem of all police states (socialist schools), along with so many other emblems of all police states? This book explains the origin of the USA's police state; why the problem continues to grow; and how to protect yourself from it.

A common example of a police state is Germany under the National Socialist German Workers Party ("Nazis"). The Nazi salute and Nazi behavior originated in the USA's Pledge of Allegiance in government schools (socialist schools). The pledge began in 1892, decades before its influence reached Germany and Adolf Hitler. The pledge was written by an American socialist as part of a conspiracy to impose government (socialist) schools, and spread the prison planet throughout the USA and worldwide.

Government schools (socialist schools) are part of the prison planet, including the police state in Germany (under Hitler's socialism) and in the USA. The USA's government/socialist schools teach students to refer to Germany under Hitler as the "Third Reich" even though Hitler did not refer to his socialist state as the "Third Reich." Many scholarly books use the unscholarly phrase "Third Reich" and fail to explain that Hitler eschewed the phrase.

Hitler did not create the phrase "Third Reich," and never used the term in his notorious book "Mein Kampf." The historian Dr. Rex Curry was the first to point out that Wikipedia (at the time this was written) and other so-called sources (including "historians" and every news outlet that you pay attention to) cite no example of the term "Third Reich" used by Hitler ever. Yet those sources repeat the phrase "Third Reich" as if Hitler repeated it daily in speeches and in print.

The inference should be that Hitler rejected "Third Reich." He never used it in "Mein Kampf," even though he DID use the word "Reich" (in reference to Germany's government) many times (over 190 times?). "Reich" was commonplace in Germany before Hitler. Wouldn't Hitler have used the phrase "Third Reich" often if his goal was to replace the plain old "Reich" that he mentioned over 190 times in his book?

Hitler banned the use of "Third Reich." During the summer of 1939, the press was directed to use the terms "Nationalsozialistisches Deutschland" (National Socialist Germany), "Großdeutsches Reich" (Greater German Reich), or simply "Deutsches Reich" (German Reich) to refer to the German socialist state in place of "Drittes Reich" (Third Reich) (Schmitz-Berning, Cornelia (2000). Vokabular des Nationalsozialismus. Walter de Gruyter GmbH & Co. KG, 10875 Berlin, pp. 159-160. (in German)). The people who would proofread Hitler's socialist press were grammar Nazis.

The phrase "Third Reich" was coined by Arthur Moeller van den Bruck (1876-1925), author of a book with the phrase for its title: "Das Dritte Reich" (The Third Reich). The book was published in 1923, giving Hitler years to consciously decide not to use "Third Reich" in Hitler's 1925-26 book "Mein Kampf." Moeller did not support Hitler nor Hitler's socialism (Moeller died in 1925, before voters from government schools -socialist schools- put Hitler into government).

It is interesting to note that the "Third Republic" in France ended with the fall of France to German socialism in 1940. The French Third Republic also bore a fasces symbol prominently in the center of its emblem.

It can be argued that the USA remains in its "Third Reich"

16

stage, following its Second Reich (the period during the War for Southern Independence), and thereafter under the dictates of American National Socialists, including Francis Bellamy and Edward Bellamy, that continues to haunt the USA today.

Dr. Curry was the first to point out that Wikipedia (and other so-called sources, including all the news outlets that you pay attention to) cites no example of the term "Nazi" or "Fascist" or "Third Reich" used by Hitler as a self-identifier in German or in any language. And yet Wakipedia (similar to all the news outlets and "scholars" that you have listened to your entire life) deceives users into believing that Hitler over-used the term "Third Reich" and "Nazism" and "Fascism" as self-identifiers. Those terms are over-used by news outlets, scholars, and by pseudonymous writers who post on the bulletin board called "Wikipedia." The Orwellian over-use of those terms is done to hide the word that Hitler DID use: SOCIALISM.

Hitler self-identified as a socialist throughout his book "Mein Kampf," and repeated (over 170 times?) the words "socialism" and "socialist" in a glowing manner. His oral presentations were similar.

This book dissects socialism under Hitler and reveals amazing discoveries (from the work of the historian Dr. Rex Curry and his colleagues at the Dead Writer's Club), including:

1. Mein Kampf does not contain the word "Nazi" in any form.

2. Mein Kampf does not contain the word "Fascist" ever as a

self reference by Hitler.

3. Mein Kampf does not contain the phrase "Third Reich."

4. Mein Kampf does not contain a single use of the word "swastika."

5. "Nazis" did not call themselves "Nazis" and they did not call their symbol a "swastika."

6. Swastikas represented crossed "S" letter shapes for the word "SOCIALIST" under Hitler.

7. VW (Volkswagen), SS, SA, & NSV and other emblems are alphabetical symbols, and show that the swastika was used as an alphabetical symbol too.

8. Nazi salutes and Nazi behavior originated from the USA's Pledge of Allegiance to the flag.

9. The Nazi salute came from the military salute (because the military salute was used in the original Pledge of Allegiance).

10. The Nazi Holocaust was part of a larger socialist Wholecaust with a much bigger death toll.

11. Vienna, Austria (Hitler was born in Austria) is the origin of the word "wiener." It is related to these phrases: Vienna

18

sausages and wiener schnitzel. But in Vienna, they don't call them "wieners," they call them "Frankfurters." Hitler liked Vienna. "Vienna" appears ~80 times in "Mein Kampf."

12. The word "Fascist" is related to the word "faggot."

13. The word "Kampf" in Hitler's "Mein Kampf" is related to these words: champagne, campaign, champignon, champion, champ, camp, and campus.

Why is there so much ignorance about Adolf Hitler, Mein Kampf, and the dogma behind them? One reason is that no one reads PRIMARY sources when studying the topics.

Primary sources are hidden by government schools (socialist schools) in the USA because they do not want Americans to learn the pledge's putrid past, including new shockers uncovered by Dr. Curry:

(1) The Pledge of Allegiance was the origin of the Nazi salute and Nazi behavior.

(2) The Nazi salute came from the military salute due to the use of the military salute in the original Pledge of Allegiance.

(3) The Swastika, although an ancient symbol, was also used to represent crossed "S" letters for "socialism" under Adolf Hitler's National Socialist German Workers Party (Nazis).

(4) Hitler transformed his own signature to appear as a stylized "S" letter reflecting the shape of the swastika symbol and his dogma of socialism.

Another discovery revealed by this book is the widespread ignorance about the revelations enumerated above.

There are many books about Hitler, or Nazism, or the Pledge of Allegiance. All books about Hitler, Nazism, or the pledge reveals that the authors overlooked all the disclosures enumerated above. How were those writers blind to the preceding discoveries? Their ignorance spans more than a century (if the years are counted from 1892, the year that Bellamy's pledge was published), or it spans more than half a century (if the years are counted since World War II and Hitler's reign).

Many people (including "scholars") have written about Hitler's Schutzstaffel (the "SS Division") and its stylized "SS" symbol. Some authors have noted that the "SS" symbol uses runes that correspond to the letter "S" as alphabetical symbolism for the word "Schutzstaffel." All of those authors failed to compare the "SS" symbol to the swastika symbol, and failed to discover the alphabetical symbolism of the swastika for "socialism" under Hitler.

Why did it take so long to uncover the facts enumerated in this book? And why do news outlets continue to perpetuate ignorance about the Pledge of Allegiance and about this exposé?

One explanation for the ignorance is: government schools (socialist schools) will not teach the truth about Francis Bellamy and the Pledge of Allegiance. Bellamy abetted those two major hallmarks of the police state in the United States (hereafter the "USA") and its constant growth: (1) Government (socialist) schools; (2) The Pledge of Allegiance.

Bellamy wanted gunvernment to take over schools. Bellamy achieved "equality" by making everyone (including "news" reporters) equally stupid via government schools. Government's schools are never going to tell the truth about him and his pledge. If they taught the truth, then no one would perform the pledge (other than weirdos).

The pledge represents a threat of violence. People were persecuted, beaten, jailed, and lynched for defying the pledge in the similar rituals in the USA, Germany, and worldwide. The pledge continues to inspire bullying and persecution. The topic intimidates journalists as it has intimidated so many other people.

News journalists remain too brainwashed and frightened to inform their readers. Their news outlets will not publish photographs or film recordings of the early pledge's Nazi salute. They will not write about the photos and films showing the early gesture.

Experiments were performed in which news reporters were asked to publish photographs and films of the early pledge salute and to examine its influence on Germany and other countries. All of the journalists refused.

The same journalists were accused of being dishonest

cowards. They continued to refuse any coverage of the issues in this book. Of those same journalists, none disputed the conclusions in this book. The experiment has also been performed by the Pointer Institute for Media Studies. Anyone can replicate the experiment.

All of the above is more proof that the USA is a police state. Journalists demonstrate that the pledge is effective obedience training. Reporters spend careers glorifying lies from public officials. It is Stockholm Syndrome. Bellamy's scheme worked.

That is why government schools are unconstitutional: They violate the First Amendment right to freedom of speech and freedom of the press. Government schools (socialist schools) tell everyone what to think and say and write. The Pledge of Allegiance is a part of that.

Twelve years of Bellamy's schools prevent newspapers, TV, and radio outlets from telling the truth. Journalists lack understanding of private property rights, supply-and-demand pricing, laissez-faire economics, free markets, individual rights, and capitalism.

Government (socialist) schools prove, by their generations of existence, and by their continued existence, that they do not work. They failed to teach people how to handle their children's education without government. They do not even attempt to teach such a lesson. They teach that government schools must always grow in size, scope, and funding.

Every popular "problem" trumpeted by politicians, media, and government is their confession that government schools never worked and must end. For example, minimum wage laws are a confession by government that socialist schools failed to produce students who are able to obtain jobs that pay more than the minimum wage. All "news" stories are such a confession: racism, violence, drugs, theft, crime, prison populations, discrimination, wage gap, recycling, eating disorders, STD's, unwanted pregnancies, obesity, militarization. Yet all popular "problems" are trumpeted for more government, more laws, more programs, and not for reducing or ending socialist schools.

The Bellamy dogma of "Christian Socialism" renders government (socialist) schools unconstitutional as an establishment of religion and as a violation of freedom of religion. Separation of church and state cannot exist where, as in the U.S., the state is your church. Because of Reverend Francis Bellamy, coerced prayers and hymns never stopped in government schools (socialist schools); The Pledge of Allegiance is the daily prayer / hymn.

An old cliche states: History is written by the victors. It would be more accurate to state: History is written (and taught) by the government. In government's schools (socialist schools) the government glorifies itself as a hero, and not as the universal monster.

Government makes the worst sociopathic serial killers seem angelic in comparison. How do their death tolls compare? Presidents, Members of Congress, governors, and state politicians are glorified in schools. Homicidal thoughts from the socialists Stalin and Mao are taught, even glorified, in universities and schools. Government officials are psychopathic arsonists who hallucinate that they are heroic firemen. Government schools give voice to serial killers, murderers, thieves, frauds, sociopaths, and other criminals.

Harry Browne, the best-selling author, said that the greatest mistake in history was letting the government educate our children. The iconoclast Dr. Rex Curry said: "Remove the pledge from the flag; remove the flag from schools; remove schools from government."

2. FRANCIS BELLAMY: UGLY FRIEND

Francis Julius Bellamy (May 18, 1855 to August 28, 1931) was born in Mount Morris, New York; however, his parents moved to Rome when Bellamy was five years old. That was the city of Rome in the state of New York (not in Italy).

In the house of his parents, and while residing in Rome (NY), Bellamy was educated at a school known as the "Rome Free Academy" (RFA). The Rome Free Academy continues to operate in Rome, NY. The RFA's school logo includes two fasces symbols.

Bellamy's connection to Rome, NY, is important because it was the origin of the "ancient Roman salute" myth (that the stiff-armed gesture is an ancient gesture from the Roman Empire) that was debunked by Dr. Curry.

Because Bellamy was from Rome, NY, the term "Roman salute" was used to refer to the gesture for Bellamy's Pledge of

Allegiance (both the original gestures and the stiff-armed gesture - the classic Nazi salute - that developed from Bellamy's original gestures).

People from the city of Rome in the state of New York were referred to as "Romans" during Bellamy's life (and they continue to refer to themselves as "Romans" today). One example of that is the headline: "Roman Lived to See U.S. Adopt Famed Flag Salute" from the Utica Observer newspaper (August 28, 1936). Another example is from 2015: "Here are the backgrounds of some notable New York Romans, past and present -FRANCIS BELLAMY..." (from the Observer Dispatch newspaper in Utica, NY on Aug. 4, 2015). As time went by, some confused people believed that the "Roman salute" referencing the city in New York, was instead a reference to ancient Rome in Italy.

Bellamy continues to reside in Rome, NY. He is buried in the Rome cemetery.

The early stiff-armed gesture in the USA's Pledge of Allegiance was not an ancient Roman salute. There was no such thing as an "ancient Roman salute" (unless one counts the middle finger salute, mentioned by Suetonius and Martial). The modern Roman salute myth evolved from the USA's Pledge of Allegiance.

Many cities in the state of New York have names reminiscent of classical history (Albany, Ithaca, Syracuse, Troy, and Utica), and that is why New York is the "Empire State" with the "Empire State Building" because it is a reference to the time period of the ancient Roman Empire.

As Bellamy's Nazi salute spread, so spread his government (socialist) schools, and so spread the use of the fasces symbol to represent socialism.

The "Rome Free Academy" school that Bellamy attended continues to operate in Rome, New York, and the school's logo includes two fasces. The official seal of the United States Senate (adopted 1886) includes a pair of crossed fasces. Two fasces appear on either side of the flag of the United States behind the podium in the United States House of Representatives. The fasces style is used in the Lincoln Memorial (the fronts of the chair's arms shaped to resemble fasces). A fasces is on the bronze George Washington statue (1882) in front of Federal Hall National Memorial in Manhattan, New York City. The fasces appears on the U.S. dime from 1916. The fasces style (as a bundle of arrows) adorns the U.S. quarter (1932) and resembles the emblem on the hat worn by Mussolini in a notorious photograph.

Mussolini was so impressed with the Roman and socialist themes in the U.S. that he honored Rome, NY with a statue of the "Capitoline Wolf" (upon which the fabled Romulus and Remus are shown suckling. It represents the socialist goal of every human suckling at the public/government teat -the wolf). The peculiar statue stands in front of The Beeches Inn in Rome, NY, where it is adorned with a plaque displaying a fasces and the phrase "New Rome." Mussolini made similar gifts to Cincinnati and to Rome in the state of Georgia (in 1931). An engraving on one of the statues reads "Anno X" ("Year 10" in Latin), referencing Mussolini's tenth year in power. In Georgia, a bronze plate on the statue prominently displays the fasces symbol. Romans believed that the father of Romulus, the mythical founder of Rome, was Mars, the god of war, and that belief would abet the dogma of "military socialism," including the Bellamy version).

Mussolini learned the Bellamy salute when he was a powerful socialist leader. No "ancient Roman" influence (real or imagined) was mentioned by Bellamy, nor by James Upham (the person who assisted Bellamy in creating the Pledge's gesture), in their descriptions of how the Pledge and its salute was written.

Francis Bellamy never used the term "ancient Roman salute" when describing his pledge's salute.

The phrase "Roman salute" did not exist at the time that Bellamy and Upham worked on the pledge (Dr. Curry's work is supported by the Oxford English Dictionary in this etymological regard). The concept/term "ancient Roman salute" was dreamed up decades after Bellamy wrote the pledge of Allegiance.

Francis Bellamy clearly explained that his pledge began with a military salute that was then extended out toward the flag. In practice, the second gesture was performed palm-down with a stiff-arm when the military salute was merely pointed out at the flag by bored children forced to do Bellamy's programmed chanting daily in government schools. That is how the straight-arm salute developed from Francis Bellamy's Pledge of Allegiance and its use of the military salute (and how the USA's pledge salute led to the Nazi salute).

An instructor at George Mason University (GMU) wrote a short item for the American Philological Association (APA) questioning whether the so-called "ancient Roman salute" ever occurred in any Roman art or text. The item noted that the salute occurred in early silent films: the American "Ben-Hur" (1907), the Italian "Nerone" (1908), "Spartaco" (1914), "Cabiria" (1914). The earliest film – Ben Hur- had at least three directors, of which two had been born and raised in the U.S. That means they attended schools where they were likely forced upon threat of violence to perform the American Nazi salute and intone the pledge on cue daily. One director was from Canada, but had moved to the U.S. at a young age and lived in the U.S. long enough to observe the bizarre U.S. practice toward the flag before he and the other directors incorporated it into the film "Ben Hur."

All film examples of the early American Nazi salute are mild compared with the daily grind of government schools brainwashing children from 1892 to perform the gesture (with robotic chanting) under threat of violence for 12 years of their lives. Adults were also forced to perform the gesture at events.

In response to the APA blurb about the GMU teacher, Dr. Curry publicly announced his discovery that the original U.S. flag salute (1892) pre-dated and inspired the use of the gesture in the later films. The pledge's early Nazi salute had been unknown to the GMU instructor when he wrote about the films.

The GMU teacher went on to author a confusing book that was debunked by Dr. Curry before it was published. He does not dispute Dr. Curry's discovery that Pledge of Allegiance was the origin of the Nazi salute and Nazi behavior. GMU's instructor mentions neo-classical artwork by Jacques Louis David, but he does not state that David's Horatii was the origin of the Roman salute myth. He states that Horatii is the "starting point for an arresting gesture that progressed from oath-taking to what will become known as the Roman salute," which actually states nothing, and is an apparent reference to his own "starting point" for writing his book. He does not contend that the painting was the origin of the Nazi salute, nor that it was the origin of the "ancient Roman salute" myth.

Hitler enjoyed American movies and had his own private cinema. The documentary "Hitler's Private World: Revealed," shows him talking animatedly about his love for cinema (his tastes included Mickey Mouse). He also teased Eva Braun about a screening in his cinema at the Berghof, and he stated, "I understand you didn't like the movie last night. I know what you want. You want Gone with the Wind."

The GMU teacher's book seems written to evade any comparison of Bellamy's socialism to the socialism touted by Mussolini and Hitler.

The book leaves readers with suspicion that the GMU teacher is unaware that Hitler and his supporters called themselves "socialists"; that Hitler's symbol represented "S" letter shapes for "socialism"; that the "Nazis" did not call themselves "Nazis"; that "Nazis" did not call themselves "Fascists"; that "Third Reich" was not one of Hitler's slogans. Is the GMU ignorant or is he intellectually dishonest in covering up what Hitler's supporters called themselves: SOCIALIST?

The GMU teacher quoted the untrustworthy book "Hitler's Table Talk" and Hitler's alleged statement: "I'd read the description of the sitting of the Diet of Worms, in the course of which Luther was greeted with the German salute." The GMU teacher had no idea what the quote references. Another amazing discovery by Dr. Curry is that the quote refers to "Luther at the Diet of Worms" (1882) by the Belgian painter Émile Delperée.

The GMU teacher also quoted Hitler's alleged statement: "It was in the *Ratskeller* at Bremen, about the year 1921, that I first saw this style of salute." The GMU teacher was unaware that, about 1921, Ernst Hanfstaengl moved from the USA to Germany and instructed Hitler on propaganda rituals that were used in America. Hanfstaengl heard for the first time a speech by Hitler in a beer hall. According to the author John Toland (p. 128 of his biography of Hitler), the first encounter between Hitler and Hanfstaengl was on 22 November, 1922 at the Kindlkeller, a large L-shaped beer hall. Hanfstaengl as the importer (and/or promoter) of the American Nazi salute is likely.

The GMU author was debunked also by Michelle Borg at the University of Sydney: "The author first turns to the early form of the Pledge of Allegiance, which originally included an entirely similar gesture to the one that came to be used by Fascists and Nazis. This uncomfortable association is not explored in depth; [He] simply asserts that the gesture had no political or historical connotations in the United States."

Borg's criticism applies to Wikipedia too, depending on the date and time that a person views Wakipedia.

How can anyone ignore more than a century of hypnotic brainwashing in government schools in the USA, boy scouts and girl scouts, modern Olympics, other sporting events, political rallies, parades and more? How does anyone ignore the persecution, bullying, and violence used to dictate the gesture and the mechanical chanting? How is it ignored today?

Fictitious Roman scenes in early silent movies only added to the "Roman" salute myth that developed from the Pledge of Allegiance (and the pledge preceded those films by more than a decade).

That the myth of the "ancient Roman salute" did not exist when Bellamy wrote his pledge (and for decades thereafter) also means that the concept of the "Roman salute" did not even exist when Jacques-Louis David painted his "Oath of the Horatii." Thus David was NOT thinking of a real or imagined "Roman salute" when he painted the Horatii, nor did David ever use the term "Roman salute" (again also see the Oxford English Dictionary).

The Horatii lie (that the Horatii painting was the origin of the "Roman salute" myth) is a very recent lie. It first appeared on Wikipedia (~2006) after Dr. Curry's discovery that the Pledge of Allegiance was the origin of the Nazi salute. The Horatii disinformation was deliberately fabricated by a liar to cover-up Dr. Curry's discovery that the pledge was the origin of the Nazi salute, to cover up the pledge's putrid past, and to side-step the influence of American socialists (e.g. Edward Bellamy, Francis Bellamy) and the USA's pledge upon German socialism and socialism worldwide.

Research produces no examples in history of anyone asserting that the Horatii painting was an example of an ancient Roman salute, nor that it inspired the "Roman salute" myth. For example, the painter Armand-Charles Caraffe, in his painting "The Oath of the Horatii" (in 1791) did not mis-interpret David's 1784 painting as an "ancient Roman salute."

In David's Horatii painting, three brothers are reaching for weapons with their fingers separated (and the two figures in back are reaching with their left hands).

The same liar who created the Horatii deceit had, until he was debunked, previously claimed that the stiff-armed salute was an actual ancient Roman salute, and he posted the lie that Roman statues displaying "adlocutio" (a gesture made by a person speaking) showed "the ancient Roman stiff-armed salute."

Wikipedia continues to mislead readers about the "ancient Roman salute" lie in articles that vary in quality from "confusing" to "deceptive." Liars on Wakipedia are similar to journalists in the old media: They will not write about the pledge's influence on socialism in Germany and elsewhere, and they will delete any information in that regard. They also do not dispute the information in this book (they merely suppress it).

The newly substituted Horatii falsity has been mindlessly

repeated by many people (as the adlocutio lie was repeated and still is) because wakipedia glorifies itself as an encyclopedia, even though it is merely an anonymous bulletin board where anyone can post anything.

It should be needless to say (but for wakipedia) that Bellamy was not influenced by Jacques-Louis David's painting "Oath of the Horatii." According to Bellamy, his pledge's gesture resulted when he was with James Upham and Upham specifically suggested gestures for the pledge that Bellamy had penned. Upham suggested the military salute followed by the arm outstretched with the palm upward (which was similar to saying "Here is the flag").

It was the use of the military salute (at the beginning of the original Pledge of Allegiance and then extended outward toward the flag) that resulted in the classic Nazi-style gesture.

From the pledge's breech birth in 1892, the stiff-armed gesture grew in popularity and was used during meetings of fraternal organizations, including the Masons. Bellamy and Upham were Masons and they both specifically promoted the use of the pledge (and its straight-arm salute) by fraternal organizations and by the Masons.

The American Nazi salute spread beyond of the USA's pledge when it was adopted for robotic chanting to state flags. Texas imposed its state "Pledge of Allegiance" in 1933. The 1933 description of the flag was extremely detailed and included precise instructions for the colors of the stripes, blood red, azure blue, and white, were said to impart the "lessons of the Flag: bravery, loyalty, and purity." In the same year that

34

German socialism achieved dictatorship, Texas imposed the American socialist Nazi salute to its flag of "white purity" in a manner reminiscent of Hitler's description of his flag in Mein Kampf. Soon thereafter, in 1935, Georgia imposed the American Nazi salute and mechanical incantation to its state flag. Rhode Island beat them all when it imposed the American Nazi salute for its pledge to the state's flag in 1910 (its source was the State Department of Education). The Nazi-style behavior continued and now 17 states have a formal pledge or salute to state flags (Kentucky, Ohio, North Carolina, Louisiana, South Dakota, Oklahoma, Mississippi, Michigan, South Carolina, New Mexico, Virginia, Arkansas, Georgia, Tennessee, Texas, Alabama and Rhode Island). It is extremely difficult to find any photographs or film footage of the early state flag salutes of Texas, Georgia, or Rhode Island.

Germans learned American behavior via old films, WWI, news reels, and the widespread use of the straight-arm salute by Germans who had studied or lived in the USA; via Americans who also studied or lived in Germany; via German-American groups in the USA (including the German-American Bund); via the Boy Scouts (who spread both the American Nazi salute and also the swastika symbol); via the official Olympic salute (another exposé by Dr. Curry is that the "official Olympic salute" was the USA's Nazi salute from the Pledge of Allegiance).

From 1892 through 1942, public officials (including U.S. presidents, congressmen, governors, state legislators and everyone down to the local dog catcher) performed the

American Nazi salute. In 2015, news outlets reported secret home movie footage from 1933 showing the "Nazi salute" performed by Edward the VIII and the future Queen Elisabeth (at seven years old). No American news reporter was aware that public officials in the USA performed the gesture from 1892 through 1942.

Before WWII, it was not illegal for citizens of the USA to support the National Socialist German Workers' Party or Hitler's political campaigns.

The National Socialist German Workers' Party (NSGWP) began in 1920, achieved electoral breakthroughs in 1930, imposed dictatorship in 1933, and invaded Poland in 1939 as allies in socialist imperialism with the Union of Soviet Socialist Republics in a pact to divide up Europe, spreading World War II, and leading to the socialist Wholecaust (of which the Holocaust was a part).

The pledge's stiff-armed salute existed from 1892 (three decades before the NSGWP) and continued in the USA throughout the existence of the NSGWP. It was the origin of the Nazi salute.

So the question remains unaddressed by Wakipedia, the old media, et cetera: which possibility had more influence: (1) The Horatii painting, or (2) decades of robotic performing of the gesture for the Pledge of Allegiance in and out of government schools (socialist schools) with threats, expulsions, persecutions, beatings, arrests, and even lynchings for those who refused (because mechanical chanting is considered so important)?

If teachers had begun each day (from 1892) by holding up the Horatii painting and commanding students to mimic it or be punished, then that would be persuasive evidence. But that is not what happened.

Did socialists in Italy and Germany fail to witness for decades the required daily robotic intonation in the US schools that was seen by German and Italian families that came and went from US schools, parades, sports, public meetings, events?

Did they also miss anything about the pledge ritual in newspapers, newsreels, movies, WWI, and WWII? Did they miss all the public officials from city, county, state, and federal, who grew up ~1892 and thereafter (including presidents, congressmen, etc) who performed the gesture and hypnotic chanting publicly? Where are those photos and films today of the old pledge gesture and public officials performing it? Did any Germans or Italians ever see those, or did the USA's Pledge of Allegiance never have any impact on anyone, anywhere, at anytime? Not even one Italian was ever aware of it? Not even one German was ever aware of it? Is that the position of wakipedia, the old media, and the GMU writer? If they concede that the pledge must have had some influence on someone, somewhere, at sometime, then who, where, and when? How much?

Why is it so important for them to cover up for the pledge and its putrid past?

They could point to earlier depictions of people holding their arms in the air, and they could declare all of them to be

37

the "ancient Roman salute" (even depictions that pre-date Rome) and it would be equally as wrong. Try Egypt. Or examine some prehistoric cave drawings.

Here is a quiz regarding these two salutes (they are invited to pick "A" or "B" as the best answer to the questions that follow below):

A. The German use of the stiff-armed gesture under the socialist Hitler.

B. The Italian use of the stiff-armed gesture under the socialist Mussolini.

Question 1: which use was more well-known at the start of the modern Olympics in 1896?

Question 2: which use was more well-known when the first film studios were built in 1897?

Question 3: which use was more well-known at the turn of the century on January 1, 1900?

Question 4: which use was more well-known during World War I (1914-1918)?

Question 5: which use was more well-known immediately before Mussolini gained power in Italy?

Of course those are all trick questions because the question's topics pre-date (sometimes by decades) the two answers. But the situation changes by adding another choice for the answer:

Here is a quiz regarding these three salutes (they are invited to pick "A" or "B" or "C" as the best answer to the questions that follow below):

A. The American use of the stiff-armed gesture under the socialist Bellamy's Pledge of Allegiance.

B. The German use of the stiff-armed gesture under the socialist Hitler.

C. The Italian use of the stiff-armed gesture under the socialist Mussolini.

The socialist Bellamy created the Pledge of Allegiance in 1892. The answer to questions 1 through 5 is "A" from the three choices: The American use of the stiff-armed gesture under the socialist Bellamy's Pledge of Allegiance.

Here is another question: which of the three uses above (A. B. or C.) lasted the longest? Most people answer incorrectly that the Hitler salute lasted longer because Hitler died later than Mussolini, and the U.S. Congress amended the flag code in 1942 so that it no longer mentioned the extended-arm gesture. But the question is a trick because all Americans did not immediately follow the flag code. Some did not want to follow the flag code. The long-standing use of the stiff-armed salute in the USA persisted for more than a decade after 1942.

Robotic chanting to the flag on cue in government schools (socialist schools) continues to this day, along with persecution for students who refuse (although the gesture was changed to hide the pledge's putrid past).

Here is the "life-span" of the gestures:
1. Socialist Bellamy ritual 1892-1942 (and beyond, even beyond WWII. And the pledge lives on today).
2. Socialist Hitler ritual 1922?-1945.
3. Socialist Mussolini ritual 1919?-1943.

As the figures show, the Socialist Bellamy's salute had about three decades of more impact preceding the Socialist Hitler salute and the Socialist Mussolini salute. It also outlived them.

Wakipedia, the old media, and the GMU writer all expose their own dark side: they love the pledge and want to divert attention to the old "irrelevant" arm gesture. The topic is actually about more than the mere gesture; the topic is about government repeatedly mandating a mechanical ritual of robotic chanting on cue in government schools (socialist schools) and at the command of government officials. Wakipedia, the old media, and the GMU writer like the ritual and its abuse of children in the USA today. They focus on the mere arm gesture in order to cover up the real problem: the modern police state ritual and their love of it. The bigger problem is the authoritarian ritual that was borrowed by German socialists, and that continues daily in the US, and that they continue to support in the US. They will not talk about their role in that.

3. EDWARD BELLAMY: BELLICOSE MILITARIST

Francis Bellamy was cousin and comrade of Edward Bellamy (March 26, 1850 to May 22, 1898). At the age of 25, Edward contracted tuberculosis (TB), and it would eventually end his life. He suffered TB's effects throughout his entire adult life. Around 1879, he abandoned the daily grind of his journalism work, and pursued literary work with fewer demands upon his health.

In 1888, after years of study and suffering, Edward's literary work led to the publication of "Looking Backward," an international bestseller.

Ten years later (1898), in his hometown of Chicopee Falls, Massachusetts, Edward Bellamy died at 48 years of age from TB. His lifelong home was designated a National Historic Landmark in 1971.

There are many parallels between Bellamy's socialism and

his other disease, TB. TB was called "consumption" because it seemed to consume people with long relentless wasting. Bellamy caught TB in his twenties. Bellamy might have caught TB while living in Germany (infra) where he also caught his socialism illness.

Tuberculosis was used as a metaphor for political decay by the socialist Adolf Hitler in his book "Mein Kampf" over two decades after Bellamy's death.

Tuberculosis remains one of the most deadly and common major infectious diseases today in developing countries that suffer under socialism. It infects two billion people or one-third of the world's population. Nine million new cases of disease, resulting in two million deaths, occur annually, mostly in backward socialist countries with bad sanitation, where no "industrial revolution" has been allowed to occur because of socialism. The number of deaths compares with the number of deaths under the socialist Wholecaust (of which the Holocaust was a part).

Edward's book "Looking Backward," spawned "Nationalism" clubs worldwide (including Germany). Both Bellamy boys were self-professed socialists who supported the movement, its "Nationalist" magazine, and the Nationalist Educational Association (the NEA -named to deliberately mimic the National Education Association in the USA).

Francis Bellamy used his position with the National Education Association (NEA) to promote "military socialism" -the dogma that he touted with his cousin. In 1892, Bellamy became chairman of the National Education Association's

43

executive committee for a National Public School Celebration plan that would lead to Bellamy writing the larger program that contained the smaller part known as the "Pledge of Allegiance."

The Bellamy "Nationalism" movement was so large that in 1935, Colombia University surveyed the scholars Edward Weeks, Charles Beard, and John Dewey regarding the most influential books and they all ranked Edward Bellamy's book "Looking Backward" (1888) nearly as influential as Karl Marx's "Das Kapital" (1867). Back then, they intended that as a compliment, not as a condemnation.

Although the German philosopher Marx published his book "Capital" in 1867 (the year before Edward Bellamy's trip to Germany), it was not translated into English until after 1886 (ideas in "Capital" had been promoted in newspapers and pamphlets in English. Marx's "Communist Manifesto" had been published in 1848).

Marx's Communist Manifesto was printed initially only in German, even though the prelude announced it was to be published in English, French, German, Italian, Flemish and Danish. After Marx's death in 1883, Friedrich Engels authored prefaces for five editions between 1888 and 1893. Among those is the 1888 English edition, translated by Samuel Moore. It has been the standard English-language version.

The distribution and influence of the English translation of "Capital," and of the main English translation of "The Communist Manifesto" both coincided with Bellamy's book of 1888.

44

German apologist Marx's "Communist Manifesto," and German apologist Hitler's socialist manifesto "Mein Kampf," and American apologist Bellamy's "Looking Backward" share many similarities, including pompous attitudes about the lives of others, and child-like concepts of economics.

Bellamy's book touted "Military Socialism" and the "Industrial Army" at the same time that Marx's Communist Manifesto touted the "Industrial Army" (and it is mentioned in Capital). Both books urged that government schools (socialist schools) be imposed in order to enforce the "Industrial Army" and socialism.

From 1868-1869 Edward Bellamy spent a year in Dresden, learned to speak and write German, attended lectures and studied German socialism. While Bellamy was in Germany, many unions were formed, and so was the German People's Party (Deutsche Volkspartei). Edward's brother Frederick wrote that Edward's letters to him were full of German socialism which "he had read and studied much at home." (see Sylvia E. Bowman "The Year 2000").

In November of 1888, Edward Bellamy hired an interpreter to translate "Looking Backward" into German (see the biography by Arthur Morgan, p. 65). In 1891, German-language editions of Bellamy's book were advertised in the USA, proclaiming that the novel "Lays the foundation of the Nationalist Movement." The German translation not only promoted National Socialism in Germany, it also promoted National Socialism in America and cultivated those Americans who later supported the USA's German-American Bund

45

movement that supported German National Socialism. The advertisements coincided with the "Nationalist" magazine of Edward Bellamy, published by the "Nationalist Educational Association."

A weekly publication that promoted Bellamy ideas was combined in advertisements with the book "Capital" by Marx as a package deal (see The New Nation, 1891-94. Marx's book was the translation by Dr. Edward Aveling).

Advertisements listed together the books of Karl Marx, Edward Bellamy, and Charles Bellamy (another one of Edward Bellamy's brothers).

The writer Gail Collins stated: "...far more American workers read Looking Backward than ever made it through Marx..." (Tomorrow Never Knows, The Nation, Vol. 252, Issue # 2, January 21, 1991).

Merritt Abrash described the Bellamy philosophy as Marxism Americanized (see Looking Backward: Marxism Americanized, In M.S. Cummings & N.D. Smith (Eds.)., Utopian Studies IV (pp. 6-9). Lanham, MD: University Press of America (1991).

The book "Edward Bellamy Abroad" by the author Sylvia E. Bowman states that Edward Bellamy's book was translated into every major language including German, Russian, and Chinese. Bowman's book is 543 pages long, and details the Bellamy inspiration to socialists worldwide.

Bowman's book devotes an entire chapter (55 pages) to describe Edward Bellamy's influence in Germany, including the years leading up to the formation of the National Socialist

German Workers' Party (Nazis). Despite her examination of Bellamy's life, Bowman is another example of an author who failed to make the discoveries made by Dr. Curry and described in this book.

Hitler was a big supporter of the Nationalist movement. In "Mein Kampf," he uses the words "Nationalist" and "Nationalism" many times (over 45 times?) and states in words reminiscent of Francis Bellamy pledge program: "The spirit of nationalism and a feeling for social justice must be fused into one sentiment in the hearts of the youth. Then a day will come when a nation of citizens will arise which will be welded together through a common love and a common pride that shall be invincible and indestructible for ever."

Edward Bellamy's Nationalist Clubs published newspapers, including one entitled "The Arena." The author Timothy Kubal, in "Cultural Movements and Collective Memory: Christopher Columbus and the Rewriting of the National Origin Myth," states that in 1891 Francis Bellamy promoted socialism in an article entitled "Socialism versus anarchy," published in the Arena newspaper.

The book "The Pledge of Allegiance" by Dr. John W. Baer states that in the Pledge of Allegiance, Francis Bellamy is expressing the ideas of his first cousin (Edward). Francis was a vice president of the Christian Society of Socialists, affiliated with Edward's Nationalist movement (Francis worked as a lieutenant in the campaign to impose their "military socialism" upon the entire U.S. economy).

The book "Looking Backward" (by Edward Bellamy) was

47

written in 1888 and described a fantasy about life in the year 2000. It is a totalitarian society where all private transactions are outlawed; where the government places all men in an "industrial army" (a Bellamy phrase) explicitly modeled on the military; where the government has taken over all schools as a government monopoly for the "industrial army" system to achieve "military socialism" (a Bellamy phrase); where everything is nationalized. All in this paragraph was portrayed as a utopia. The Bellamy cousins admired the military, and said it was very efficient, and they wanted the military system to be imposed upon all of society.

The Bellamy dogma continues to be promoted by the "Edward Bellamy Memorial Association." The association owns and occupies his home at 93 Church St, Chicopee, MA 01020. The association operates part of the house as a museum, renting out the other to obtain financial support.

Edward Bellamy's house is used by another group that continues to support the Bellamy dogma: the Theosophical Society (TS), a group created by Helena Petrovna Blavatsky from Russia, the leading theoretician of Theosophy who claimed to be an occultist and a spirit medium. The TS group exists in other locations, including Saint Petersburg, Florida, and internationally.

4. PLEDGE OF ALLEGIANCE DRILLS

Francis Bellamy's Pledge of Allegiance was published first in the Youth's Companion Magazine in 1892. That article shows the following: The original pledge began with a military salute for the phrase "I pledge allegiance...." and then the right-arm military salute was extended outward toward the flag for the rest of the pledge so that the right arm was held aloft at an angle directed at the flag, as if to signify, "There is the flag."

The following paragraph is an excerpt showing the pledge as printed for the first time in the 1892 edition of the Youth's Companion Magazine:

At a signal from the Principal the pupils, in ordered ranks, hands to the side, face the Flag. Another signal is given; every pupil gives the Flag the military salute - right hand lifted, palm downward, to a line with the forehead and

close to it. **Standing thus, all repeat together, slowly: "I pledge allegiance to my Flag and the Republic for which it stands; one Nation, indivisible, with Liberty and Justice for all." At the words, "to my Flag," the right hand is extended gracefully, palm upward, towards the Flag, and remains in this gesture till the end of the affirmation.; whereupon all hands immediately drop to the side.** [end of excerpt]

The impact of the military salute as the origin of the Nazi salute is visible in old film footage of children performing the Pledge of Allegiance. Film footage shows conclusively that the military salute was, in practice, extended straight outward to point at the flag (with the palm down).

The original Youth's Companion article along with other research led to more discoveries by Professor Curry:

(1). Due to the way that the pledge used the gestures sequentially, the military salute led to the Nazi salute. The Nazi salute is an extended (outstretched) military salute. Although the original Youth's Companion description directed that the palm be turned upward, that was not the case in practice. Historic photographs and film show that in practice the palm was down because the pledge was performed casually with the initial military salute perfunctorily stretched straight out toward the flag (palm down, because the military salute is palm down in the USA -but it is not palm down in the British army and in some other countries).

(2). The straight-armed salute of the original Pledge of Allegiance was the source of the salute of the National Socialist German Workers' Party (Nazis).

(3). The gesture was neither an ancient Roman salute nor an ancient Olympic salute, and was not ancient in any way.

(4). Photographs and films show that eventually the military salute was dropped entirely from the chanting ritual. Perhaps teachers and parents were disturbed by the military part, if not by the whole pledge. Perhaps it was considered disrespectful to the military – a euphemistic was of saying it was creepy to have children pretending to be in the army. When the military salute was abandoned, it left nothing but the classic Nazi salute.

The above explains why the media, schools, history museums, and other so-called "educational" outlets, will never show film footage (nor photographs) of the early Pledge of Allegiance. Due to general political considerations, they do not want to show the pledge's putrid past (and its putrid present, and its putrid future).

5. THE CIVIL WAR & MILITARY SOCIALISM

Which is more similar to the swastika flag: the Confederate flag or the U.S. flag? Which is more of a symbol of racism?

The Confederate flag is a popular answer in government schools (socialist schools), with students who are ignorant of the history of the U.S. flag, its Pledge of Allegiance, and the Bellamys.

That answer changes when students learn that the U.S. flag and its Pledge of Allegiance were the origin of the Nazi salute and Nazi behavior (e.g. robotic chanting). It was also the origin of the Nazi salute and Nazi behavior under the swastika flag.

The government (socialist) schools that Bellamy promoted imposed segregation by law and taught racism as official policy. Those racist policies even outlasted German national socialism. Some critics argue that official segregation and

52

racism continues today in the socialist schools, albeit in different forms.

Within the racist schools, segregated classrooms of black children were forced to perform the Nazi salute and to chant mechanically en masse at the ring of a bell for 12 years of their lives. People who refused were expelled, beaten, imprisoned, and even lynched. It is impossible to quantify the damage that was done and that continues to be done as a result of socialist racism.

Even after some school segregation ended the government continued its racism and used forced busing to destroy black neighborhoods.

The U.S. continues to hold the worst world records for imprisoning blacks and otherwise ruining their lives with felony convictions for victimless crimes and fabricated arrests.

Nondiscrimination laws make it illegal for businesses to say they won't hire Mexicans, but immigration laws make it actually impossible to hire almost any of them - even if Americans want to hire them and they want to work - just because they happen to have been born in Mexico. Of course, the same official discrimination and segregation is mandated against the Chinese, and the Irish, and the other seven billion people on earth.

Francis Bellamy and Edward Bellamy admired how the military had killed so many Americans during the War for Southern Independence. It was the source of their Nationalism and their national socialism. The phrase "one nation indivisible" in Bellamy's pledge reveals his perception of the war: not against slavery, but to reverse the South's declaration of independence in order to "preserve the union."

After the War of Northern Aggression, the pledge enabled Christian Socialists to lead a daily witch hunt for disloyalty within government schools (socialist schools) each morning at the ring of a bell.

Bellamy did that despite the history that is celebrated each 4th of July: when slaveholders seceded from their country (Britain) and soon thereafter waved the red, white, and blue flag over their seceded slave-holding rebel land.

Bellamy wanted everyone to chant his Pledge of Allegiance to the nation and its flag - a flag that had flown over a nation of slavery since the flag's creation so long ago.

Confederacy groups begin their meetings with the Pledge of Allegiance to the U.S. flag.

The U.S. flag resembles the First Confederate national flag (not the Confederate battle flag with the "X" letter shape of the St. Andrew's cross). The first Confederate national flag contained three horizontal stripes of equal height, alternating red and white, with a blue square two-thirds the height of the flag as the canton. Inside the canton are white pointed stars of equal size, arranged in a circle, pointing outward, and representing the seceded states. As secession spread, the flag contained thirteen stars representing thirteen seceded states (similar to the thirteen seceded states and stars on the original flag of the United States).

Today, whenever the First Confederate national flag is flown (instead of the Confederate battle flag), students from

54

the government's schools do not know what the flag is. If the First Confederate national flag replaced the Confederate battle flag, years would pass before most students from government schools understood what the flag was and that a substitution of flags had occurred.

Southerners in the Confederate States of America (CSA) believed they embodied the ideals of the American Revolution, and the earlier secession in 1776.

Abraham Lincoln's Gettysburg Address said the soldiers sacrificed their lives "to the cause of self-determination - that government of the people, by the people, for the people should not perish from the earth." H.L. Mencken said: "It is difficult to imagine anything more untrue. The Union soldiers in the battle actually fought against self-determination; it was the Confederates who fought for the right of people to govern themselves."

The German socialist Karl Marx (with the International Workingmen's Association a.k.a. the First International) wrote a letter congratulating Lincoln upon Lincoln's re-election. Marx, the man who inspired the worst mass slaughter of humanity in history, praised Lincoln, the man who presided over the worst mass slaughter of Americans in history. Marx's letter was written between November 22 & 29, 1864.

Socialism, as touted by the International Workingmen's Association, attracted many thousands of supporters throughout the USA. The large immigration of German workers had a big impact on the politics of the North in the twelve years before the War of Northern Aggression.

The German socialist Hitler also praised Lincoln in Mein Kampf: "[T]he individual states of the American Union . . . could not have possessed any state sovereignty of their own. For it was not these states that formed the Union, on the contrary it was the Union which formed a great part of such so-called states" (page 566?).

The Soviet socialist Stalin joined with the socialist Hitler in a pact to spread their socialism by violently taking over other states, and forcing others to remain within their control.

Those tactics had germinated in 1848 when Karl Marx and Friedrich Engels wrote The Communist Manifesto (published in German on February 21, 1848). The "Demands of the Communist Party in Germany" (March 1848) demanded the unification of Germany (In 1848 there were many sovereign states - Empires, Kingdoms, Grand-Duchies, Duchies, Free Cities, et cetera, - in the German Confederation. They had descended from the settlement at the Congress of Vienna held in 1815 at the end of the French Revolutionary and Napoleonic wars).

Lincoln and socialism inspired Francis Bellamy and Edward Bellamy. The Bellamy comrades wanted everything to be taken over by government. The pledge of servility put everyone on the road to serfdom. They are one of the origins of modern feudalism, crony socialism and the military-socialism complex. Edward Bellamy's internationally best-selling socialist book "Looking Backward" portrayed their goal as a utopia.

The Bellamys wanted the government to take over all

schools as a government monopoly in order to create the "industrial army" system to achieve "military socialism" (a Bellamy phrase). The Bellamys touted "military socialism" (the phrase they used to describe their dogma) because they so admired how the military destroyed the South. They wanted the military system imposed on all of society.

The Pledge of Allegiance is a slave's pledge of allegiance to his master.

The pledge continues to be a daily witch hunt for disloyalty within government schools (socialist schools) at the ring of a bell. Each morning, kids drink the Kool-Aid.

6. HISTORY OF MASONS

Francis J. Bellamy and James Bailey Upham (the person who assisted Bellamy in creating the Pledge of Allegiance) were both Freemasons. Bellamy was a Mason in Little Falls Lodge No. 181, in Little Falls, NY (and a genuine Masonic Lodge website, the Grand Lodge of British Columbia and Yukon, openly and proudly boasts of his membership in Freemasonry). James Bailey Upham was a Mason in the Converse Lodge in Malden Massachusetts (Also see "Twenty-Three Words" by Margarette S. Miller).

Edward Bellamy's father-in-law was a Baptist minister who'd been forced out of his church for becoming a Freemason.

Freemasonry fit the Bellamy dogma of "military socialism." Regimentation and ritualism appealed to Masons like Francis Bellamy and James Upham. Freemasonry touts an intricate mythology, veiled in allegory, and manifested by pledges, uniforms, symbols, and rituals.

Within the Masonic order, Upham was a Knights Templar, the most esteemed and discriminating order. The word "discriminating" is a double entendre in that the Knights Templar is the only Masonic order that excluded (and still excludes) non-Christians (people they classify as Jews, Muslims and atheists), according to the book "To the Flag" by Richard J. Ellis (another book about the pledge that fails to ask or answer the question of the pledge as the origin of the Nazi salute).

The Order of the Knights Templar, also known as the American Rite, is the highest order in the York Rite, the largest Masonic organization in the United States. According to the book "The Pledge of Allegiance" by Dr. John W. Baer, it is equal to a Thirty-Third Degree Scottish Rite Mason, the top of the Masonic hierarchy.

The Masons also exclude women and there is a separate "auxiliary" organization that accepts women and it is called the "Order of the Eastern Star" and its symbol is a star turned upside down.

Bellamy was a bigot. Bellamy's racism is shown in many examples, including these: "Where every man is a lawmaker, every dull-witted or fanatical immigrant admitted to our citizenship is a bane to the commonwealth," and "Where all classes of society merge insensibly into one another every alien immigrant of inferior race may bring corruption to the stock," and "...there are races which we cannot assimilate without lowering our racial standard, which should be as sacred to us as the sanctity of our homes."

Bellamy wanted the government to take over all schools in order to stamp out individuality and force everyone to be the same (that is what Bellamy and other socialists meant by "equality"). When the government granted his wish, the socialist schools imposed segregation by law and taught racism as official policy.

The 1925 film "The Vanishing American" depicts segregated Native Americans being taught the Nazi salute and Bellamy's robotic chanting in a government school. An infamous photograph that is available on the internet shows African American children performing the Nazi salute and chanting Bellamy's Pledge of Allegiance in their segregated socialist school. Another infamous photograph shows segregated Japanese Americans performing the American Nazi salute in an internment camp during another one of Franklin Delano Roosevelt's many socialist programs or pogroms (the photograph is by Dorothea Lange, a photographer who worked for the ominously titled Resettlement Administration (RA); for the FERA (forerunner of today's FEMA); for the FSA; and under the auspices of the USDA).

During Bellamy's time (and today?), the Knights Templar and Masons in general lamented what they called capitalism's crass commercialism, selfish materialism, and excessive individualism. That view fit nicely with the socialist views of Upham and Bellamy.

That anti capitalist view also fit Hitler and is expressed in

60

Mein Kampf.

"Mein Kampf" is usually translated into English as "My Struggle," however it could also be translated as "My Campaign," because Kampf is related to the word "camp" in the sense of a battlefield, a field, or an encampment, and is related to the following words: champagne (grapes from a field), campaign (war), champignon (mushrooms from a field), champion (battlefield victor), champ, camp (field setting), and campus. "Mein Kampf" is about Hitler's struggle for (his campaign) for socialism.

"Mein Kampf" refers to Freemasonry multiple times and always in a critical or disapproving manner. Nevertheless, Freemasonry was involved in the formation of the Nazi Party. That involvement included Rudolf Glandeck von Sebottendorff (born Adam Alfred Rudolph Glauer in 1875) and Hermann Pohl (founder of the fraternity, the German Order Walvater of the Holy Grail).

Sebottendorff had been initiated into the Rite of Memphis, a Freemason group. Sebottendorf and Pohl established a fraternity in Munich known as the "Thule Gesellschaft," on August 17, 1918 (see "Anti-masonry Frequently Asked Questions," Section 6, version 2.9, of the Grand Lodge of British Columbia and Yukon). It was originally called the "Studiengruppe für germanisches Altertum" (Study Group for German Antiquity).

On January 5, 1919, the Thule group merged with the Committee of Independent Workers, renaming themselves the Deutsche Arbeiter-Partei (the German Workers' Party). Adolf

Hitler claimed he was the seventh member to join this group and he changed its name to the National Socialist German Workers' Party in 1920.

Sebottendorff authored the novel "Der Talisman des Rosenkreuzers" (The "Rosicrucian Talisman," and the "Rosicrucian" combines the words "rose" and "cross").

Another of Sebottendorff's books "Bevor Hitler Kam" ("Before Hitler Came" 1933) was banned in Bavaria. That book stated that Hitler was influenced by the Thule Gesellschaft.

The Thule dogma was influenced by occultists such as Lanz von Liebenfels (1874-1954 and a promoter of Ariosophy), Madam Helena Blavatsky (who also used the swastika symbol to promote Theosophy), and Guido von List (1848-1919). List's pet words (Ariosophy, Aryan, Armanist) all evoked his occult socialist ideas of an aristocracy of enlightened leaders and List's central goal of a super socialist man, or the superior socialist society.

In 1899, Lanz founded his Order of the New Templars, and the name was inspired by the Knights Templar. In his related magazine "Ostara" he used the swastika symbol as well as the kruckenkreuz (aka croix potent). Lanz' magazine was noticed by Hitler. In 1934, a year after Hitler came to power, Lanz claimed that the Order of the New Templars was the "first manifestation of the [German National Socialist] Movement..."

There are photographs of James Upham that show him wearing the uniform of the Knights Templar. Although

Upham, Bellamy, and other Masons criticized crass commercialism and capitalism as part of their socialist ideology, they enjoyed sashes, gloves, belts, swords, plumes, and other rich regalia.

While Upham and the Bellamys promoted "military socialism," the Masonic uniform at that time (as worn by Upham) was modeled after the military and included various medals and badges that were similar to those adopted later by the National Socialist German Workers' Party.

One of the symbols is called a Maltese Cross and others are what the Nazi's called the "Ritterkreuz" (Rider Cross, Knight's Cross or Iron Cross).

It is doubtful that any Mason today would still wear Upham's uniform publicly because those symbols became almost as notorious as the swastika (Hakenkreuz or "hooked cross") under the National Socialist German Workers' Party.

The Freemasons suffer faults that are shared by other civic groups. A review of web sites for most civic groups reveals no understanding of private property rights, supply and demand pricing, laissez-faire economics, free markets, individual rights, and capitalism.

A review of most civic groups reveals vague altruistic clichés that translate into active support for expanding government and various socialist schemes.

Freemasons begin meetings with the Pledge of Allegiance today. They do it because of Francis Bellamy and James Upham, both Freemasons and both socialists, who created the original 1892 chant.

63

Bellamy and Upham took advantage of the vague socialism of the Freemasons (and similar civic groups) to spread their dogma. It continues to happen even though the original straight-arm salute has been replaced.

In the past, the Masons excluded people that they defined as "negroes, mulattoes or women." The groups in many states would not admit people they classified as "cripples."

While freedom of association is an important right, those types of policies are pernicious when people support government institutions, because government institutions are utilized to impose such policies by force of law. That is what happened in the USA.

In the USA, the Bellamy and Upham dogma supported a government takeover of education in order to have children mimic the military and to produce an "industrial army" (a Bellamy term). The government's schools imposed segregation by law and taught racism as official policy. The USA's behavior was an example for three decades before the Nazis.

American socialism was similar to German socialism at that time because Jehovah's Witnesses, blacks, and the Jewish, and others attended government schools that dictated segregation, taught racism, and punished children who refused to perform the straight-arm salute and mechanical chanting of the Pledge of Allegiance to the flag. There were acts of violence. There were incidents in which government schools attempted to take children away from parents on the grounds of "unfit parenting" if the parents would not force the children to chant the pledge and perform the gesture.

64

— Libertarian History —

When Jesse Owens competed in the 1936 Olympics in Nazi Germany he performed the initial part of the American gesture to the flag (the military salute part), but did not perform the straight-arm gesture, as he did not want the gesture to be misunderstood as a salute to Adolf Hitler. Other photographs show U.S. athletes performing the American stiff-armed salute (the classic Nazi salute) at the Olympics in 1936 and at earlier Olympic games. The 1936 Olympics exemplifies how the American Nazi gesture had spread outside of the pledge itself, and was being used as a general salute during the U.S. national anthem and the anthems of other countries.

In the past, the U.S.'s Nazi gesture had been adopted as the Official Olympic salute, and the Olympics had helped to spread the U.S.'s gesture globally.

In 1936, many of Owens' fans in the U.S. attended (and had attended) segregated government schools where the pledge was performed with the straight-armed gesture, and where they were required by law to chant it mechanically on command in government schools (socialist schools). The U.S. practice of official racism and segregation in government schools even outlasted the Nazi Party after its defeat in WWII, and into the 1960's and beyond.

In 1936, the military salute alone (as performed by Jesse Owens at the Olympics) was not the customary civilian salute to the U.S. flag. The 1936 Olympics and the war that followed all added to the 1942 interference by Congress regarding the flag ritual at that time. Congress eventually eliminated the military salute, and also eliminated the straight-arm salute.

Congress legislated in favor of the hand-over-the-heart. The gesture was not officially altered by Congress until 1942, after the beginning of WWII. That is when the modern hand-over-the-heart was enacted into law.

The Mason's had (and have?) a practice of discriminating against many people to exclude them from their groups, but they did not exclude Germans.

It is important to remember that during all that time, German-American Freemasons attended racist and segregated government schools in the U.S. and saluted with a straight-arm salute toward the U.S. flag, as written by the self-proclaimed national socialists (and Masons) Francis Bellamy and James Bailey Upham. That was a long time before (and leading up to) the adoption of the salute by the National Socialist German Workers' Party.

The National Socialist German Workers' Party was influenced by German-Americans who were already national socialists in the United States. Some German-Americans joined the German American Bund movement (Deutsch-Amerikanischer Volksbund) to support national socialists in Germany before WWII. The bund began as the Friends of New Germany in Chicago in 1933. This group traced its roots to the Teutonia Society and National Socialist Party, both active in the USA during the 1920s.

There was much travel between the U.S. and Germany (the Hindenburg zeppelin disaster occurred in 1937 in New Jersey).

7. AMERICA GOES TO GERMANY

In "Mein Kampf" Hitler never mentioned the stiff-armed gesture.

The notorious gesture used by German socialists and American socialists was never referred to as the "Roman salute" by Hitler. The term "Roman" appears many times in Mein Kampf (along with various other references to ancient Rome and various uses of the word "Rome"), but the phrase "Roman salute" never appears as a description of the notorious stiff-armed salute, nor as any other description.

There are infinite ways in which German socialists learned the American socialist salute.

From 1892 through 1942, public officials (including U.S. presidents, congressmen, governors, state legislators and everyone down to the local dog catcher) performed the American Nazi salute and were photographed and filmed doing

67

so. Those photos and films are rare because people don't want to know the truth. Public officials in the USA who preceded the German socialist (Hitler) and the Italian socialist (Mussolini) were sources for the stiff-armed salute (and hypnotic chants) in those countries and other foreign countries.

A specific possible source of the gesture for Hitler was President Woodrow Wilson during World War I. Socialist leaders in the USA (e.g. Wilson) were using the gesture before socialist leaders in Italy and Germany aped them (along with robotic chanting in unison on command in government schools (socialist schools)). President Wilson insisted that all school children recite the pledge, and he led them into doing so using the American Nazi salute. After World War II, the Bellamy salute that Wilson so loved became less popular. The mechanical incantation on command continued daily (with an altered hand gesture), and it haunts children to this day.

Another specific source for Hitler learning the stiff-armed salute and mechanical chanting from the United States would be Ernst "Putzi" Hanfstaengl, one of Hitler's intimates, who attended schools in the USA.

During the time that Hanfstaengl was attending school in the USA, the straight-arm salute was used for various purposes, including: the National Anthem (the Star Spangled Banner); by American athletes during Olympic games and other sporting events; for school flags; and even as a general greeting, or for cheering during sports events (including Harvard football games).

About 1921, Hanfstaengl moved to Germany and heard for

the first time a speech by Hitler in a beer hall. Hitler stated that the first time he saw the straight-arm salute he was in a beer hall and he described it as occurring at "about" the same time (as when Hanfstaengl claims that Hanfstaengl heard Hitler speak in a beer hall). According to the author John Toland (p. 128 of his biography of Hitler), the first encounter between Hitler and Hanfstaengl was on 22 November, 1922 at the Kindlkeller, a large L-shaped beer hall. Hanfstaengl as the importer is also consistent with the untrustworthy "Hitler's Table Talk" quote: "It was in the *Ratskeller* at Bremen, about the year 1921, that I first saw this style of salute." Hanfstaengl as the importer (or promoter) of the American pledge's Nazi salute is likely.

Of course, there were other Germans, et cetera, who had moved to and from the United States since 1892 (the start of the stiff-armed salute's use for the national flag). There were also movie depictions and other ways in which Germans would have been exposed to the early American raised-arm gesture.

Rudolph Hess published an article titled "The Fascist Greeting" in June 1928, claiming that German socialists used the gesture as early as 1921, before they had heard about the behaviors of the socialist Mussolini.

8. SWASTIKAS = "S" SHAPES (SS, VW)

The swastika was a popular symbol in the United States during the time that the Bellamy cousins were promoting their "industrial army" under their "military socialism" in their government schools (socialist schools) with their Pledge of Allegiance.

American soldiers used the swastika as their symbol early in World War I, and up to 1941, against Germany. The symbol was used by Americans in the French Escadrille Lafayette; by the 45th Infantry Division; and on Boeing P-12 planes. The symbol was used by the Krit Motor Car company (based in the USA) on vehicles exported to Europe and used in World War I.

An American postcard pre-dating World War II, and circa 1915 (World War I) shows the swastika joined with the U.S.'s flag. The postcard reads "May our glorious flag and this 'lucky star' guide you and keep you wherever you are." The swastika is the 'lucky star' under the U.S.'s flag. At that time, the flag was worshiped with the Nazi salute under threat of prosecution in schools that imposed segregation by law and taught racism as official policy.

Boy Scouts in the USA wore medals bearing the swastika and performed the Nazi salute for the Pledge of Allegiance and adopted (as did Girl Scouts) America's Nazi salute as their own salute. The British handbook "Scouting for Boys" (p. 27 of the 4th edition, London 1911) displays the scout swastika badge and states, "A scout on seeing a person wearing this badge will go up, salute, and ask if he can be of any service." Most people who read that sentence will not realize that the salute is the American Nazi salute, to be performed upon seeing the swastika. Scouts traveled internationally to spread their paramilitary practices and American military socialism. Was German socialism an evolution of "Lord of the Flies" with Boy Scouts gone bad?

A Freemasonry group -the Grand Lodge of British Columbia and Yukon- displays on its website a photograph of what it identifies as a Navajo Indian carpet (circa 1925) decorated with the Freemason symbol between two swastikas. That Freemason site also boasts that Francis Bellamy, author of the Pledge of Allegiance, was a Mason. The site neglects to mention anything about the pledge's early Nazi salute and influence.

The swastika was also used by the Theosophical Society (TS), an international group that promoted the socialist

71

schemes of Edward Bellamy, along with odd racial theories (using the term "Aryan"). The leader of TS, Helena Blavatsky, used a "seal" (emblem) as early as 1875 that included a swastika at the top of seven symbols (for seven races). The swastika was in the classic "Nazi" style (on one point, as if drawn in a diamond, and in the "S" letter orientation). In 1888, Blavatsky's book "The Secret Doctrine" (bearing the swastika seal) stated: "Mankind is obviously divided into god-informed men and lower human creatures. The intellectual difference between the Aryan and other civilized nations and such savages as the South Sea Islanders, is inexplicable on any other grounds." She used the term "Aryan" in a way that is a reminder of its etymological relationship (from Greek aristoi for "noble") to these words: aristocrat, aristocracy, Ariosophy, Aristotle, arch, Iran. Blavatsky, from Russia, was influential there, and claimed to be from an aristocratic family.

In 1917, socialism was imposed in Russia (renamed the Union of Soviet Socialist Republics). The first new paper money (rubles) after the socialist revolution displayed swastikas in the same "S" letter style that later became the symbol of German socialism.

At the turn of 1918-19, and unmentioned in "Mein Kampf," Hitler wore a red brassard and supported the short-lived Bavarian Soviet Republic (or Munich Soviet Republic), according to Thomas Weber in the book "Hitler's First War."

Mein Kampf mentions Kurt Eisner, "Soldiers' Councils," and that time period.

There is something important that is not in Weber's book: Perhaps the Bavarian Soviet Republic experience played a role in the German National Socialist leader (Hitler) adopting a swastika symbol that had been used as a symbol of socialism by Soviet socialists on ruble currency (in 1917 and 1918).

The Bavarian Soviet Republic provides more evidence that Adolf Hitler used the swastika to symbolize crossed "S" letters for "socialism" under his National Socialist German Workers Party.

As the First World War (1914-1918) drew to a close, Germany began to follow Russia into more socialist revolution. The German Revolution or November Revolution occurred in 1918 at the end of the First World War. In August 1919 it resulted in the establishment of what later became known as the Weimar Republic (1919-1933 and named after Weimar, the city where the constitutional assembly took place). During this period, and well into the next era of National Socialism, the official name of the state was the German Reich (Deutsches Reich). The conditions which gave birth to the German revolution were similar to those in Russia in 1917 (resulting in Soviet socialism). Thereafter, sustained socialist agitation and strategy was pursued by many socialists including the socialist Hitler and his National Socialist German Workers Party. Germany's path included the abdication of Kaiser Wilhelm II and led to the socialist Hitler.

On March 27, 1917, German socialists helped Vladimir Lenin (and 32 other socialist fellow travelers) ride by train through Germany to Russia to impose socialism there and demand an end to the war with Germany. Lenin was a loony follower of the demented German socialists Karl Marx and Friedrich Engels.

November 1923 brought another attempt at socialist revolution in Germany by Hitler. It resulted in his imprisonment where he wrote Mein Kampf, a book that drones on about his socialist plans. Hitler was released from prison in December 1924.

Hitler collaborated with Soviet socialists again in 1939 when German socialists became allies in socialist imperialism with the Union of Soviet Socialist Republics in a pact to divide up Europe, invading Poland together, spreading World War II, and leading to the socialist Wholecaust (of which the Holocaust was a part).

German socialists and Soviet socialists reunited again in East Germany from 1949 to 1990. The motto of East Germany became "Workers of the world, unite!" (the motto that had been on early Soviet paper ruble currency before Hitler expanded Germany's socialism). Some German swastika-style symbolism was popularized by Soviet socialists in the form of the "S" shaped logo used on the notorious Trabant Sachsenring car. The Schutzstaffel ended under German socialism and the Stasi began under Soviet socialism (with a fascinating repetition of the "S-S" sound shared by the swastika).

The socialist Adolf Hitler participated in three attempted violent socialist revolutions" (but he succeeded in imposing socialism via voters electing him to office).

The following are Hitler's three attempts at violent socialist revolution (two were at Munich and those two were only four years apart) -

1. Munich Soviet Republic 1918-1919 (aka Bavarian Soviet Republic) - under Kurt Eisner. German socialists conspired with Soviet socialists to spread the Soviet socialist "revolution" into Germany.

2. Munich Beer Hall Putsch - 1923 (November 8-9, 1923). Hitler was arrested for his socialist activities, and was charged with treason, in connection with the Munich Beer Hall Putsch. Imprisoned, Hitler wrote his socialist manifesto "Mein Kampf."

3. Poland 1939 - German socialists and Soviet socialists became allies in 1939 in a pact of socialist imperialism to divide up Europe, spreading WWII, and leading to the socialist Wholecaust (of which the Holocaust was a part), the worst slaughter of humanity in history. Hitler and German socialists touted international socialism in a conspiracy with Soviet socialists.

Concerning the Munich Soviet Republic, Hitler had suspiciously little to say in Mein Kampf or ever. An excerpt: "In the course of the new revolution of the Councils I for the first time acted in such a way as to arouse the disapproval of the Central Council. Early in the morning of April 27, 1919, I was to be arrested..." Another excerpt: "A few days after the liberation of Munich, I was ordered to report to the examining commission concerned with revolutionary occurrences in the Second Infantry regiment." There is nothing about his reasons for staying in Munich, nothing about the horrors of the councils (soviets) which he actually knew, nothing about the severe fighting that preceded the liberation of Munich. A photograph exists that seems to show Hitler at Kurt Eisner's funeral procession.

While in jail for his second attempted socialist revolution (the Beer Hall Putsch), Hitler wrote Mein Kampf which promotes socialism (by the very word "socialism" repeated over and over by Hitler) from beginning to end. Hitler always used the term "Socialist" to describe himself and his dogma, and he did not refer to himself as a "Nazi," nor as a "Fascist," nor did he use the term "Third Reich." Those latter terms are used today by socialists to cover-up what Hitler and his supporters called themselves: SOCIALISTS.

According to Mein Kampf, Hitler immersed himself in Marxist studies.

Hitler also adopted as his notorious symbol the very same symbol that was used on the first paper money of the Union of Soviet Socialist Republics. Hitler used the Soviet socialist symbol to represent crossed "S" letters for his own socialism under the National Socialist German Workers Party

Eisner and the Munich Soviet Republic used a solid red flag for the "socialist revolution." Hitler used the red flag too, and place his crossed "S" letters for "socialism" upon his red banner.

Hitler also adopted the notorious stiff-armed salute that originated in the USA's Pledge of Allegiance to the Flag, authored by the American National Socialist Francis Bellamy

It is fascinating to see how almost all so-called historians refuse to describe the Beer Hall Putsch as an attempted violent socialist revolution, even though that is exactly how Hitler perceived it and described it.

Historians warn 'Hitler said exactly what he was going to do in Mein Kampf! We must not forget!" And then the history books actively hide what Hitler said in Mein Kampf, and afterward.

German socialists did not refer to their symbol by its popular modern name, "swastika." They called it a "Hakenkreuz." The term "Hakenkreuz" means "hooked cross." To Germans at that time, the Hakenkreuz symbol was a type of domestic (German) cross, not a foreign Sanskrit "swastika." That is one reason why the German term "Hakenkreuz" (hooked cross) is covered up with the word "swastika" today.

The deception creates comical confusion: The German Women's Order supplied nurses for wounded socialists through its branch, the "Red Swastika" (at least that is how the name is often referred to in English books about German socialism), and described as the "Nazi version of the Red Cross." Readers who are familiar with books about the work of the historian Dr. Rex Curry know that in German it was not called the "Red Swastika." It was called the "Rot Hakenkreuz" (red hooked cross) which other English writers translate as "Red Swastika" and compare it to the "Red Cross," which would be an obvious

77

comparison (it IS an obvious comparison to German speakers) if those English translators called it the "Red Hooked Cross," instead of using the misleading "Red Swastika" translation. The translation game is sneaky and funny.

The term "swastika" continues to be used to slander a foreign symbol in ongoing efforts to hide what German socialists thought about their symbol: that it was a type of cross and it was altered for use as alphabetical symbolism for "socialism."

The modern misnomer "swastika" was used (and continues to be used) to cover up German socialism's origin in American Christian Socialism, via Francis Bellamy and his cousin Edward Bellamy.

To put it another way, Hitler loved to wear a cross and he wanted others to wear a cross (on armbands, medals, posters and more) and he put a cross on his flag.

The double "S" letters and sounds of the word "swastika" and "socialism" were (and are) interchangeable. They are, in a sense, mutually onomatopoeic. They are linked in a way that the four letter N-word (Nazi) is not. In Hitler's stylized symbol, the swastika is synonymous with, and is a mnemonic reminder of, his socialism.

Hitler's "S" shape for the swastika added to the ignorant belief that German socialists called their symbol a swastika, in that the word "swastika" starts with the letter "S" and has two "S" sounds (and letters) in its spelling, as does the word "socialism."

Although the swastika was an ancient symbol for "good

luck" in India (and the word "swastika" is Sanskrit), that is not why it was used by German socialists.

If Hitler was aware of a general meaning of "good luck" for the symbol, then that would have encouraged him in his use of the symbol for his socialist dogma. All socialists mistakenly believe that their policies are "auspicious good luck" for everyone.

There is a question whether Hitler even knew of the term "swastika" or that the symbol was an ancient good-luck symbol in India. Additional support comes from John Toland's lengthy book "Adolf Hitler: The Definitive Biography." Toland asserts (page 86) that when the leader of the National Socialist German Workers' Party adopted the symbol, it was already in use as a symbol for another socialist group, a fact known by Hitler when selecting the symbol. Toland writes "Drexler [Anton Drexler] suggested calling their group the German Socialist Party (the same name of a similarly motivated party founded a year earlier [1916?] in Bohemia [Czechoslovakia], whose emblem incidentally, was the swastika)."

Based on Toland's book and other sources, there is a question whether the leader of the National Socialist German Workers' Party was even aware of any meaning for the symbol other than as a symbol of an existing socialist group.

Another entry in Toland's book (page 183) references the use of the hooked cross under Hans Knirsch, founder of the National Socialist Workers Party in Czechoslovakia, a group that was also known as the Sudetendeutsche National Sozialistische Partei (Sudeten-German National Socialist

Party).

If the swastika was a symbol of the Sudetendeutsche National Sozialistische Partei, then that use provides additional evidence of alphabetical symbolism for the swastika's two overlapping "S" letters: "Sudeten Socialism" or even "Southern Socialism." The word "Sudeten" came to mean "Southern" for many Germans, although the original etymology is unclear.

Toland also notes that the swastika was long a symbol of the Teutonic Knights and had been used by Lanz Von Liebenfels, the Thule Society and a number of other groups before Hitler's Socialist Party.

Another example of the swastika's use is at Lambach Abbey where Hitler attended as a youth in Austria. Revealing differences exist between the swastika symbols of Abbey Lambach, of the Thule Society, and of the symbol used later by German socialists. If the two earlier symbols influenced the later Nazi symbol, then they demonstrate Hitler's alteration of the symbols to more closely reflect overlapping "S" letters in the later Nazi symbol.

The book "Swastika: the earliest known symbol and its migrations" (1894) by Thomas Wilson shows that the symbol was used in and around ancient Germany and worldwide. The following is from Wilson's book (page 771):

"Dr. Schliemann found many specimens of Swastika in his excavations at the site of ancient Troy on the hill of Hissarlik. They were mostly on spindle whorls, and will be described in due course. He appealed to Professor Max

Muller for an explanation, who, in reply, wrote an elaborate description, which Dr. Schliemann published in the book 'Ilios.'

Professor Muller commences with a protest against the word "Swastika" being applied generally to the symbol, because it may prejudice the reader or the public in favor of its Indian origin. Muller says:

'I do not like the use of the word svastika outside of India. It is a word of Indian origin and has its history and definite meaning in India. * * * The occurrence of such crosses in different parts of the world may or may not point to a common origin, but if they are once called Svastika the vulgus profanum will at once jump to the conclusion that they all come from India, and it will take some time to weed out such prejudice.'"

Muller's prediction was amazing in its accuracy, and it is amusing that he labeled so many people in the world today as "vulgus profanum." The word "swastika" was used enough that it became the prevailing term, even as a substitute for the actual German word "Hakenkreuz" (and the English term "hooked cross") and many people concluded falsely that all such symbols, including Hitler's Hakenkreuz, were references to India's swastika.

People who want to "save the swastika" are cross about Hitler's "theft" of "their" symbol. But swastika-lovers will never explain that Hitler did not call his symbol a "swastika," and that he used it as "S" letters for "socialism." Swastika-lovers are at cross purposes in distinguishing the swastika from the symbol of German socialism.

Hitler's Hakenkreuz was not always called a "swastika" outside of Germany. In the U.S., in the UK, and elsewhere, it was also called "hakenkreuz" or "hooked cross" or "crooked cross" or "armed cross."

A popular explanation of the work of the historian Dr. Rex Curry regarding the swastika symbol is: "Although an ancient symbol, the swastika was also used by Hitler to represent crossed 'S' letters for 'socialist' under his National Socialist German Workers Party."

A common retort is: "The swastika is an ancient symbol that pre-dated Hitler by thousands of years. That common retort is proof that government schools (socialist schools) produce dimwits and must end. Government schools produce adults who believe swastikas cannot be altered in their use or appearance due to some "magic" spanning thousands of years.

Today, the term "swastika" is used to slander a foreign symbol in an ongoing effort to cover-up what German socialists thought about their symbol. The schools and the media are as unwilling to report the facts about the swastika as they are unwilling to print a historic photograph of the Pledge of Allegiance's early Nazi gesture.

A web search for "types of crosses" shows a chart of 25 collected images that include the "iron cross," "maltese cross," "florian cross," and more; but no "hooked cross" is depicted. Such charts reveal that the "vulgus profanum" who listed the "types of crosses" do not know that Hitler's symbol was a type of cross.

The same web search for "types of crosses" show other charts that include a 'swastika" that is facing in the "Z" letter shape direction (the opposite orientation of Hitler's symbol), and it is depicted as if drawn in a square (not a diamond), and it is NOT identified as a "hooked cross." Such charts are stupider than the charts mentioned in the preceding paragraph. They reveal that the "vulgus profanum" who listed these "types of crosses" are EXCLUDING Hitler's hooked cross, and are identifying the Indian/Buddhist/Hindu swastika as a "cross" in a misleading and ignorant manner, without explanation.

Before German socialism, the swastika symbol was usually oriented horizontally (as if it was drawn within a square, NOT a diamond) and was pointed left or right (see Wilson's book and illustrations therein).

During Hitler's early life, Hitler viewed the symbol pointed left or right and oriented horizontally (as if it was drawn within a square). A drawing by Hitler (he had been an aspiring artist) shows a fireplace mantel decorated with two of the symbols, both horizontal; one points left and the other points right. That use changed during the existence of the German Socialist Party. Hitler presided over the symbol's mutation. Under Hitler, the swastika became a socialist cipher, and a doppelsieg for a doppelgänger.

Hitler's modification turned the Nazi symbol 45 degrees to the horizontal (as if it was drawn within a diamond shape). The change also turned the Nazi symbol to point the arms rightward in newer, future uses. That also became the official version displayed on the flag. Both transformations to the German socialist symbol emphasized "S" shapes in the orientation.

According to Steven Heller, author of "The Swastika: Symbol Beyond Redemption?" and art director of The New York Times Book Review "Hitler's major contribution was to reverse the direction of the swastika."

But Hitler did more than merely reverse the direction. That is one of the many discoveries that Heller failed to make, including: (1) the symbol represented "S" letters for "socialism" under Hitler, and (2) the relationship of Hitler's hooked cross and his dogma to Christian socialism, to Francis Bellamy, and to the American Nazi salute from the Pledge of Allegiance.

9. HOLOCAUSTS & WHOLECAUSTS

The Bellamy dogma was the same dogma that led to the modern Christian Crusades of Christian socialism, and to history's worst bloodbath under the socialist Wholecaust (of which the Holocaust was a part): ~50 million slaughtered under Stalin and Soviet Socialism; ~40 million under Mao and Chinese socialism; ~20 million under German socialism.

Under socialism, the cross (the old Christian cross, the Crucifix, and the hooked-cross of socialism) continued to represent human sacrifice and death. The state is the only modern religion that continues to demand human sacrifices. Crucifixion is a form of capital punishment, execution, and self-sacrifice (or suicide in the case of socialism or "Christian Socialism"). Those connotations make the cross a meaningful symbol for the deadly dogma of socialism.

Critics think it is odd that Christians (and Christian

Socialists) wear crosses and crucifixes, for it would be odd if tiny firearms were worn on chains by admirers of Abraham Lincoln (the 16th President), John F. Kennedy (the 35th President), James A. Garfield (the 20th President), or William McKinley (the 25th President).

Hitler loved to wear a cross and he wanted others to wear a cross (on armbands) and he put a cross on his evil book, on his flag, and everywhere. It was the hooked cross. Old photographs and film footage show German socialists wearing crosses (e.g. hooked crosses on armbands) as they persecute Jews forced to wear the Star of David (Mogen David).

Hitler's anti-Semitism was preceded by Stalin's. Under Soviet socialism all Jewish religious practices were banned, including circumcision. "FREE" (Friends of Refugees of Eastern Europe) has helped Jews from Soviet socialism obtain circumcisions. All practicing Jews had to escape Soviet socialism (no one could leave unless permitted by the slave masters on the Soviet plantation). Stalin was worse than every Caesar, Kaiser, and Czar whose footsteps he followed.

Socialism's anti-Semitism continued in China where Mao followed the lead of Stalin and Hitler in banning all Jewish religious practices. It is fortunate that Mao had essentially no Jews to murder in China, for if he had then he might have exceeded the number of Jews slaughtered by Stalin and Hitler (in light of Mao's terrifying killing rates).

North Korea continues to impose similar anti-Semitic policies.

Mao paid homage to Hitler by bringing red armbands back

into fashionista style, along with looney chanting on cue, goose-stepping, mass murder, and Mao's equally evil book of socialism that had no buyers (without threats, and by not printing other books on the socialist presses, and by banning other books outright). Mao's socialist slaves lifted his little book in Hitler's American salute, while wearing Mao's Nazi-style red armband, and hailing Mao with similar socialist slogans.

Even so, German socialism was a third rate killing machine. It was the Third Reich in the sense of the third socialist reich under the socialists Stalin, Mao, and Hitler. Hitler came in third place behind the larger death tolls of Stalin and Mao. That makes Mussolini the "Fourth Socialist Reich" in that gang of four?

In "Mein Kampf," Hitler refers to Christian Socialism glowingly: "To-day, as well as then, I hold Dr. Karl Lueger as the most eminent type of German Burgermeister. How many prejudices were thrown over through such a change in my attitude towards the Christian-Socialist Movement!" Lueger was active in Viennese politics from 1891 (and mayor from 1895-1910), when Christian Socialism had been heavily influenced by the Bellamy boys (from 1888). In "Mein Kampf," Hitler self-identified as a socialist throughout, and repeated (over 170 times?) the words "socialism" and "socialist" in a glowing manner. Hitler's speeches were similar.

Mein Kampf rarely mentions the political concepts of "left" (5 times?) and "right" (1 time?).

In "Mein Kampf," there is no appearance of the term "Third Reich." Hitler did not create a state or any specific "Reich." In light of the fact that the word "Reich" appears so often (over 190 times? And in reference to the historic government of Germany) in "Mein Kampf," a reader imagines that Hitler would have used the phrase "Third Reich" often, if it was part of Hitler's plan. Hitler did not do so.

The inference should be that Hitler rejected "Third Reich" in "Mein Kampf" in that the phrase originated years before Hitler wrote "Mein Kampf." In 1923, the phrase "Third Reich" was coined by Arthur Moeller van den Bruck (1876-1925), author of a book with the phrase for its title: "Das Dritte Reich" (The Third Reich). Moeller did not support Hitler nor Hitler's socialism (Moeller died in 1925, before voters from government schools -socialist schools- put Hitler into government).

Dr. Curry was the first to point out that Wikipedia (and other so-called sources, including all the news outlets that you pay attention to) cites no example of Hitler ever using the term "Third Reich" or "Nazi" or "Fascist" as a self-identifier in German or in any language. And yet Wakipedia (similar to all the news outlets that you have spent your entire life paying attention to) deceives users into believing that Hitler over-used the term "Third Reich" and "Nazism" and "Fascism" as a self-identifier for his dogma. The nuts who write for Wakipedia (and its ilk) are the people who over-use those terms. They over-use those terms to hide the word that Hitler DID use: SOCIALISM.

A popular claim by socialist liars is that Hitler used the word "socialism" to trick people (socialists?) into supporting him. Those liars trick people into believing that Hitler used other self-descriptions: Nazi, Fascist, Third Reich.

The socialist Dark Ages included the modern inquisitions for much of the world: millions were tortured, interrogated and persecuted as "heretics" against socialism. Family members would denounce each other in show trials. It was much worse than the earlier inquisitions and Dark Ages. Socialists promised heaven on earth but provided hell for everyone not part of the ruling class.

The socialist Dark Ages continue in some parts of the world, including North Korea (satellite photographs taken at night of North Korea and the surrounding area show that North Korea remains in the literal socialist Dark Age). The socialist Wholecaust (of which the Holocaust was a part) continued in North Korea, where an estimated three million starved to death in the 1990s. Time Magazine reported on March 29, 2016 that the socialist government warned the population that another famine is imminent in North Korea, where the dictator (Kim Jong-un) is known as "the only fat kid in the country."

The socialist Wholecaust caused famines in Cambodia from 1975 to 1979 with 500,000 to 2 million deaths, representing ten to twenty percent of the country's total population, making it one of the deadliest famines in modern history (by percentage of the population of the country).

The socialist Wholecaust occurred under Chinese socialism in the late 1950s and early 1960s, when over thirty million perished under Chairman Mao Ze-dong's "Great Leap Forward" into famine. In the more capitalist USA, Chinese restaurants -owned and operated by Chinese- were satiating non-socialist bellies all over America (but it was deadly to dine at any overly "authentic" Chinese restaurant that adhered to Mao's food service socialism; and their fortune cookies were threatening).

Today, in the United States, Bellamy's Pledge of Allegiance continues as a daily socialist inquisition in government (socialist) schools. From its origin in 1892, the pledge remains the first bullying that begins each school day for small children up through high school graduation.

In the past, the pledge inspired beatings, arrests, school expulsions, and lynchings. E. V. Starr of Kansas was sentenced in 1918 to twenty years of hard labor for abusive language toward the U.S. flag. A federal judge felt powerless to reverse the lower state court's sentence even though the judge believed that Starr was "more sinned against than sinning." The mob that instigated Starr's persecution, he wrote in his opinion, had descended into the kind of "fanaticism" that fueled the "tortures of the Inquisition."

According to the Bellamy cousins, Jesus was a socialist and Christianity is socialism. Under that dogma, socialism (via the old Crusades) initiated the socialist bloodbath long before it was exceeded in the later socialist Wholecaust (the modern socialist Crusades, of which the Holocaust was a part).

Francis Bellamy's interpretation of Christianity is similar to "Christian atheism" - rejecting belief in the God of

90

Christianity, but embracing the supposed teachings of "Jesus the socialist." In comparison, a person is a Marxist for following Marx's ideas while not thinking Marx was a god. With that logic, the socialists Stalin, Mao, and Hitler would have been "Christians," if they believed that Christ was a socialist who wanted everyone to spread socialism. Every monster believes that, if there are gods, then the gods support him.

The Bellamy cousins believed that they promoted Our Lord and Savior "socialist government" as foretold by Jesus the socialist. Through Christian socialism, Bellamy touted an omnipotent/omniscient entity (government or God) ruling over everyone. Many people believe in a supreme power who rules beneficently over all of humanity. That is the essence of both socialism and religion. The question must be asked: How do you separate church and state when the state is your church?

Socialists are faith-healers fleecing the gullible crowds. Miracles are promised for the worship of gov via the pledge: magically "free gifts" from gov (healthcare, schools, sports stadia, and more); fiat paper money printed at will; endless socialist debt to pay for it all. It is the revelation of Edward Bellamy's utopia.

Christianity and religion are often maligned for the number of deaths they caused. Socialists are often maligned for the number of deaths they caused. Whatever those numbers are, they are combined into one number under the Bellamy dogma. According to Bellamy, Christianity was socialism. Jesus was a socialist touting the same dogma as Stalin, Mao and Hitler.

The millions killed by Stalin, Mao and Hitler were caused by the same dogma touted by Jesus and Christianity: Socialism.

Under the Bellamy dogma, Christ was to a large degree a non-religious figure whose true message was socialism. Bellamy's concept of Christianity (Christian socialism) is not inconsistent with the atheism of Stalin and Mao. Socialism is the actual message and goal, Christ was simply a messenger of socialism, similar to his modern "angels" in the socialists Stalin, Mao, and Hitler.

Hitler's "Minister" of Propaganda under German socialism was Joseph Goebbels, and his diary (dated 16 October 1928) states: "What does Christianity mean today? National Socialism is a religion. All we lack is a religious genius capable of uprooting outmoded religious practices and putting new ones in their place. We lack traditions and ritual." One of the new rituals Minister Goebbels used for propaganda was the stiff-armed salute from the "religious genius" and one-time minister Francis Bellamy, and Germany used the salute in a similar mechanical chanting fashion of worship en masse and on cue.

The author William L. Shirer in his book "The Rise and Fall of the Third Reich" suggests that German socialism logically evolved from Martin Luther to Adolf Hitler, as an expression of national character. Shirer argued that the course of German history "made blind obedience to temporal rulers the highest virtue of Germanic man, and put a premium on servility." That Sonderweg (special path) interpretation of German history was then common in American scholarship. Luther's influence applies to U.S. history via "Christian Socialism" and the Bellamy dogma.

Socialism is the opiate of the masses. Or is it religion? No matter, the two are now combined. And pledges of allegiance are Gregorian chants.

The Anarchist philosopher Larken Rose retorted: "You are not Christians. You are not Jews. You are not Muslims. And you certainly aren't atheists. You all have the same god, and its name is 'government.' You're all members of the most evil, insane, destructive cult in history. If there ever was a devil, the state is it. And you worship it with all your heart and soul."

Modern Socialist Crusades had many other similarities to the old Christian Crusades, because the modern crusades had: aggressive expansion attempts by modern socialists; all "sins" (all atrocities) are justified and forgiven to whosoever took up the cause of socialism. The crusades reinforced the connection between socialism and militarism. Similar to the old Crusades, the modern socialist Crusades were military campaigns, consistent with the Bellamy dogma of "military socialism" and similar socialist militarism under Stalin, Mao and Hitler. The modern socialist crusaders often pillaged the countries through which they invaded in the typical medieval manner. Socialists often retained much of the territory gained rather than returning it (e.g. the territories acquired by Soviet socialism under its pact of socialist imperialism with German socialism).

The Soviet-German treaty of 1939 included a secret protocol that divided territories of Poland, Romania (specifically Bessarabia), and Baltic states (Finland, Estonia,

Latvia, Lithuania) into German and Soviet "spheres of influence," anticipating potential "territorial and political rearrangements" (har, har) of these countries.

Soviet socialists and German socialists continued their imperialist pact in a "Declaration of the Government of the German Reich and the Government of the USSR of September 28, 1939," declaring their desire to "put an end" to the war of England and France against socialist Germany, and threatening England and France ominously: "in case of the continuation of the war, the Governments of Germany and of the USSR shall engage in mutual consultations with regard to necessary measures." Germany attacked France on May 10, 1940. Paris fell to the Germans on June 14, 1940. The Battle of Britain began on July 10, 1940. Hitler and Stalin remained allies until June 22, 1941.

The author Timothy Snyder extensively researched some of the socialist Wholecaust for his book "Bloodlands: Europe between Hitler and Stalin." He ranks the most common methods by which mass murder occurred under the socialist Wholecaust: (1) starvation; (2) shooting; (3) gassing. He states, "Of the fourteen million civilians and prisoners of war killed in the bloodlands between 1933 and 1945, more than half died because they were denied food," and adds, "After starvation came shooting, and then gassing." (Preface: Europe page xiv). Snyder ranks the most common methods by which mass murder occurred under the German socialist Holocaust thusly: (1) shooting; (2) asphyxiation by carbon monoxide from engine exhaust; (3) Zyklon B pesticide gassing.

Snyder's ranking of starvation as a common method of mass killing under Soviet socialism and German socialism is characteristic of socialism elsewhere, including Chinese socialism. It remains a trademark of North Korean socialism. Socialism is sociopathy.

In a speech delivered to the London School of Economics on January 21, 2014, Snyder stated that in 1938 the socialist Stalin had killed 1000 times the number of Jews killed by the socialist Hitler. That Hitler began to catch up with the Soviet socialist killing spree after Soviet socialists and German socialists became allies in their pact (1939-1941) to divide up Europe, invading Poland together, and launching the Socialist War (World War II). The German Holocaust began on territories that Soviet socialists occupied (or had occupied). That Soviet socialist citizens actively participated with German socialists in the German socialist Holocaust. Most of the perpetrators of the Holocaust were Soviet socialist citizens. That German socialists were able to draw Soviet socialist collaborators everywhere they went.

Snyder's work shows why Soviet socialism is responsible for the German socialist Holocaust (which is usually blamed only on German socialism).

In some lectures, Snyder fails to mention "socialism" even as he purports to analyze the motivations and ideologies of Hitler and Stalin. Sometimes he covers up for "socialism" by using the terms "Nazism" and "Stalinism." He perpetuates and reinforces widespread ignorance because uninformed listeners could leave his lectures without learning from Snyder that

Hitler did not refer to his party as the "Nazi Party" and did not refer to members as "Nazis." Listeners are not told that Stalin and Hitler (and their supporters) touted "socialism" in speeches and writings, by the very word. It causes other listeners to wonder if Snyder likes "socialism," and dislikes how Stalin, Hitler, and Snyder all show affection for the word.

It is a reminder of the 2016 candidate for president Bernie Sanders (BS), who self-identified as a socialist and claimed that many in his father's family were killed by "Nazis." The old media never asked: "BS, do you know that Nazis did not call themselves 'Nazis'? They called themselves the same thing you call yourself: SOCIALIST."

It is a reminder of the New York Times (NYT) writer Walter Duranty who won a Pulitzer Prize (that should be revoked) covering up Soviet socialism's horrors. Duranty suppressed the Holodomor, the mass death by starvation of Ukrainians, Tartars, Kazakhs, and other non-Russian ethnic groups in the Ukraine and the Caucuses, the south, and Siberia.

Today, the NYT continues a deceptive policy from Duranty's days that is followed by many newspapers, writers, and socialist shills: refer to German socialism as "Nazism," and refer to Soviet socialism as "Communism," and don't mention the word they both used: "Socialism"; Don't tell readers that Hitler did not self-identify as a "Nazi," nor a "Fascist," nor as the "Third Reich," but use those words to cover up the word he DID use: socialist.

Snyder's book "Bloodlands" refers to German socialists as both "Nazis" and "National Socialists." In comparison, Snyder

96

labels Soviet socialism as "Stalinism." Sometimes he uses the phrase "National Socialism and Stalinism" when he refers to German socialism and Soviet socialism collectively. Why does he not refer to them as "German National Socialism and Soviet National Socialism"; or "German Socialism and Soviet Socialism"; or "Hitler's Socialism and Stalin's socialism"?

Readers should be grateful that Snyder is more honest than other historians who hide "socialism" with the phrase "Nazism and Stalinism." Snyder writes, "Hitler called his enemies 'Marxists,' and Stalin called his 'fascists,'" even though Snyder overlooks the irony that Hitler and komrade Stalin were both doing what Snyder (and other writers) do: protecting the word "socialism."

Snyder has many foreign linguistic skills. He can cover up for socialism in multiple languages.

Snyder so desperately covers up for socialism that he refers to Hitler as an "anarchist." I am not making this up. To make matters worse, Snyder never tells his audience: "I said Hitler is an 'anarchist' even though I cannot cite any example of Hitler ever self-identifying with that term, nor using the word in any way." It seems as if Snyder would not be bothered if people started to believe that Hitler called himself an anarchist, in the same way that people incorrectly believe Hitler called himself a "Nazi," and a "Fascist." When Snyder is interviewed by people who don't seem to know Hitler's words, Snyder does not clarify for them. Snyder uses the term "Nazi" and never explains that Hitler did not use the term in Hitler's many speeches and writings in which Hitler droned on about socialism and socialists. Snyder cites no example of Hitler using the word "Nazi," nor "Fascist," nor "Third Reich," nor "anarchist" as a self description (for more on all of that see Dr. Curry's work). Hitler droned on glowingly about "socialism," as did Stalin and Mao.

The above is why Snyder did not make the historic discovery that the swastika was used by Hitler to represent crossed "S" letter shapes for "socialist" (Dr. Curry's discovery). Snyder was intellectually incapable of making that discovery. That is why Snyder will never mention the swastika's alphabetical symbolism under German socialism: for the same reason that, in interviews and lectures, Snyder avoids or minimizes any mention that Hitler and his supporters called themselves "socialists." It is important to repeat the point: Snyder will never explain to his audiences and readers that the swastika was used by Hitler to represent crossed "S" letter shapes for "socialist." It does not support his misleading narrative and his efforts to hide what Hitler said and the actual words Hitler used: socialist and socialism. Snyder does not want to talk about it.

Snyder obscures the socialist interrelationship of Hitler, Stalin, and Mao, as he hides the influence of American socialists. That is why Snyder did not make the historic discovery that the USA's Pledge of Allegiance (from the American socialist Francis Bellamy) was the origin of the Nazi salute and Nazi behavior. That is why Snyder will never educate his audiences about that.

In a telling double-standard, Snyder's anarchist "slur"

avoids the "anarchist" Stalin and the "anarchist" Mao (even though they allegedly believed that socialism would evolve to a utopian level with the "withering away" of the state -just not while Stalin and Mao were top socialist "archists" killing millions). Snyder is mum about the "Union of Soviet Anarchist Republics" (USAR) and its motto during its alliance of Soviet anarcho-socialism and German anarcho-socialism in 1939 (when they invaded Poland together, launching the anarchist war of WWII): "Anarchists Unite!"

When German socialists invaded a country, they would often cause "state destruction," according to Snyder in his bizarre explanation of "anarchist" Hitler. Snyder knows that wherever Hitler went he imposed the German socialist government. The archists Stalin, Mao, Hitler all imposed their socialist governments wherever they went (and for a while the archo-socialists Stalin and Hitler did it together). Sometimes (often? always?) they destroyed whatever government was present and replaced it with their socialist government. That is not "anarchy."

All socialism exemplifies "state destruction" and the eventual failure of the state (e.g. the USSR in 1991) because socialism causes shortages, poverty, suffering, starvation, and the deaths of millions. The Austrian economist Ludwig Von Mises (born in Ukraine) explained why in his book "Socialism: An Economic and Sociological Analysis" (1922, 1932, 1951): Socialists always impose the dual strategy of (1) nationalizing as much industry and property as possible; and (2) "destructionism," defined as "destroying the social order which is based on private ownership." Socialism is chaos.

Snyder uses socialism's bloodbath to promote yet more statism (some of that is in Chapter 4, "The State Destroyers," in his book "Black Earth"). Snyder points out the obvious: that of the states invaded by German socialists, some local governments were "destroyed" and some local governments were left intact, and survival rates were higher in the latter. Duh.

Many of the deadliest invasions by German socialism occurred in areas that were butchered first by Soviet socialism, then by German socialism, and then again by Soviet socialism.

Submitting is good? When German socialism was appeased by a state that Germany invaded, then Germany might kill fewer of that state's people. If Snyder urges capitulation to German socialism (to avoid bloodshed), then he shares another point of view urged by German socialists. That is why "states" are important, using Snyder's reasoning: so that they can embrace German socialism and thereby reduce deaths. That is disturbing.

Snyder continues with his explanation of why archy is good: Countries block and/or send back non-citizens when non-citizens try to immigrate after fleeing German socialism (or Soviet socialism). When that happens, it is better to be a local citizen than a non-citizen fleeing Soviet or German socialism. A doomed outsider is told to stay away, or is returned from whence she came, to go die somewhere else.

Snyder promotes statism with the fact that France protected its own Jewish citizens while France sacrificed Polish Jews (who had fled to France after Germany's invasion of Poland), returning Polish Jews to German socialists. Statists make creepy arguments.

Snyder worsens. He cites for support (with apologies?) the socialist police state "Nazi Germany" (Snyder's term) as proof that statism is a good thing: Jews in Germany had ~50% chance of living, while Jews in areas that Germany invaded had ~5% chance of survival (those numbers have been used by Snyder). Under socialism, you might live longer because your government might kill more foreigners than locals (i.e. you), says Snyder in defense of statism/socialism. People who support government say odd things. It will be frightening to read Snyder's cheery spin on the citizen/non-citizen death rates under the archo-socialists Stalin, Mao, Pol Pot, North Korea, et cetera.

Snyder promotes the nation state (even national socialism itself?), with its borders, visas, passports, and control over the movement of human beings; he promotes how people are treated as sheeple who are socialized property owned by fenced-in farms (their socialist states). Immigration laws are meant to keep out "undesirables." The immigration controls that Snyder praises are the same rules that continue to kill today in the same way they killed during the socialism of Germany, China, and the Soviet Union. Because of immigration laws, the same thing could happen again under another socialist war and socialist Wholecaust. Victims would be prevented from fleeing, or would be sent back. It happens today. It continues in regard to China, North Korea, Cuba, and more.

Snyder's "anarchist Hitler" ploy is misdirection to hide another embarrassing similarity between Snyder, Hitler, Stalin, and Mao: the socialists Stalin, Mao, and Hitler were archists and Snyder is too. They are not even minarchists. They are bad archists who spread malarchy. Just like the Marxists of another era, Snyder substitutes mythical thinking about the economy for loyalty to individual liberty. Snyder needs to face what he is and face the dogma Snyder touts: archy and the violence, theft and chaos it embodies.

The unmatched bloodbath of socialism inspired two new fields of study: anarchaeology and misanthropology. Anarchaeology is the study of how people throughout history have progressed and thrived with limited government (minarchy) or with no government at all. Misanthropology is the study of how governments cause chaos, and create poverty, misery and mass slaughter that destroys civilizations. Both fields consist of members (Anarchaeologists and misanthropologists) who often study the worst examples in history: the socialist Wholecaust (of which the Holocaust was a part). Modern Holocaust museums will triple in size when they include the entire socialist Wholecaust.

World War I (WW1) and World War II (WW2) were governments killing millions of people. War is when one government tries to destroy and/or replace another government. Germany's socialist government committed the same atrocities as the Soviet's socialist government and China's socialist government: they all killed millions of people.

102

WW2 was yet another archist war and was related to the archist WW1. Many nations are today engaged in ongoing militarism and warfare that is a result of the archist WW1 and WW2. Government is the most sociopathic killer of all human history. It is not anarchy. It is the opposite of anarchy.

"Hitler or Stalin: Who Killed More?" asks Snyder in another article. He confusingly argues that "Hitler" is the answer. Snyder's low numbers are from Soviet socialist sources. Why does he believe those figures? Walter Duranty was willingly duped by Soviet socialist sources.

Snyder dances around part of his "accountant" question: Did the number of people killed by Stalin in the socialist famine in Ukraine and the Caucasus (1930-33) exceed the number of Jews killed by Hitler? A clear answer is not provided. Snyder thinks it was close, apparently. Maybe he considers it a "tie" in that contest.

Snyder uses the term "non-combatants" when accounting, and he seems to include ~3 million "Soviet prisoners of war" starved (or shot) by German socialists. That figure is embarrassing and damning for Soviet socialists because they started Hitler's worst killing (and WWII) with German socialists in the so-called "non-aggression pact."

Snyder should include Hitler's death toll in Stalin's death toll (It is easy to do. It was done by the historian Dr. Rex Curry). Stalin and Hitler were in a conspiracy, the Molotov-Ribbentrop alliance between German socialism and Soviet socialism, which launched Hitler's worst destruction (including the German Holocaust). According to Snyder, most abettors in

103

the German Holocaust were willing Soviet socialist citizens.

Joachim von Ribbentrop was convicted at the Nuremberg trials for his role in the Holocaust and hanged; Vyacheslav Molotov was not. Molotov lived until 1986! After Stalin's death in 1953, Molotov staunchly defended Stalin's policies, harshly criticized Stalin's successors, and opposed "de-Stalinization." Soviet socialists helped prosecute German socialists at Nuremberg for their "crimes against humanity" (including the crimes that they committed together). Socialism is nutzi.

Other deaths that Snyder ignores via "Stalin" are deaths under Soviet socialism before and after Stalin was head of the USSR. The Soviet socialist famine of 1921 is one example, with 6 million deaths. Sometimes, Snyder restricts his death count to "Stalin vs. Hitler," lowering the numbers, as compared with the bigger body piles for "Soviet socialism vs. German socialism."

Stalin was a deadly mentor to Hitler. Stalin was a politburo member from the beginning (in 1917) of the Soviet socialist death machine. He was appointed General Secretary of the Central Committee in 1922. He consolidated power following the death of Vladimir Lenin in 1924. Stalin had a long murderous track record for Hitler to admire and aspire to. German socialists were playing catch-up.

Stalin's death toll easily includes Mao's death toll, along with Hitler's. Stalin inspired, aided, and abetted Mao, in another conspiracy, between Soviet socialism and Chinese socialism. One example: thirty million or more Chinese starved during the Great Leap Forward, as Mao followed Stalin's model of collectivization.

Stalin's death toll continued after Hitler died (1945) because Stalin continued killing until Stalin's death in 1953. Stalin's death toll continued after Stalin died (1953) because Mao continued killing until Mao's death in 1976. Soviet socialism's death toll continued after Soviet socialism died (1991) because his socialist work lived on in China (and North Korea, Cuba et cetera). Soviet socialism's corpse pile hasn't stopped growing yet.

The previous paragraph should be expanded (beyond "death counts) to include decades of robbery, slavery, torture, and terrorism that continued under Soviet socialism after German socialism ended. Snyder and other writers minimize socialism's horrifying reality by focusing on death counts.

One example is Czechoslovakia, where German socialism plundered first, and then Soviet socialism followed the path of German socialism there and for decades longer (1948-1990).

Soviet socialism's omni-crimes continue today.

Stalin's guilt for the horrors of Hitler and Mao (and others) is consistent with Stalin's (and the USSR's) stated threat to spread their violent dogma of socialism worldwide. The threat was reinforced on Soviet paper ruble currency in 1919 with the ominous motto "Workers of the world, Unite!" (other paper rubles were decorated with swastikas). The motto was repeated on the rubles in every major language, including German, Chinese, and Italian. Soviets foresaw the socialist greed and gullibility of Germany, China, Italy and other countries.

Socialists share the same genocidal goal of "class cleansing" and "ethnic cleansing." They wanted a "classless society" and their overt target was the elimination of the "capitalist class" and capitalists. They considered capitalists to be heathens under socialism. Capitalists (and other lower types) are sub-humans who must give way to the socialist "superman." In pursuit of that goal, they engaged in "ethics cleansing" - imposing government schools (socialist schools) to teach generations of children about socialism: that theft, violence, and murder are magnanimous altruism. Socialist schools (government schools) remain. The lesson continues.

When German socialism began stealing land, Soviet socialism was already far ahead in the same crimes of theft and enslavement. The USSR provided Hitler with inspiration. For a while, Soviet socialism and German socialism were co-conspirators in their crimes.

Most people have heard earfuls about where German socialism went to plunder. For comparison, the following is a list of some places (22) where Soviet socialism robbed, murdered and/or enslaved: Albania, Poland, Bulgaria, Romania, Czechoslovakia, East Germany, Hungary, Yugoslavia, Ukraine and the Caucasus, Belarus, Armenia, Georgia, Azerbaijan, Estonia, Kazakhstan, Kyrgyzstan, Latvia, Lithuania, Moldova, Tajikistan, Turkmenistan, and Uzbekistan.

Soviet socialists continued the forced colonization policies that they shared with German socialists, even after Hitler was defeated. Soviet socialism's forced settlements took several forms. A notorious example was the Gulag labor camp system of penal labor. Resettling of entire categories of population was another method of imposed under Soviet socialism. Involuntary settlement was used in the colonization of remote areas of the USSR. Soviet socialism used forced deportation where its pal Hitler had desired to use it: Ukraine.

After German socialism ended, Soviet socialism's ethnic cleansing continued. The USSR was imposing homogenous territories. Some of the casualties were ethnic Germans (as had been established at the Potsdam Conference). Many others were Poles and Ukrainians. Many millions of victims were forced onto trains and shipped elsewhere. As under German socialism, the actions had widespread support.

Socialism is modern slavery. Soviet socialism was a sad reminder of the etymological relationship of the words "slave" and "Slav." Hitler used forms of the word "Slav" and "slave" many times in his books in apparent ignorance of the relationship. The word "Slav" includes a places where many dies under Soviet socialism and German socialism: Ukraine and the Caucasus (the last word being "Slavic" and the origin of the word "Caucasian," so that the word "slave" originated from Caucasians and other Slavs who were enslaved).

The German socialist Karl Marx openly touted dictatorship and mass murder to impose dictatorship. "Dictatorship of the proletariat" was his term. "The very cannibalism of the counterrevolution will convince the nations that there is only one way in which the murderous death agonies of the old society and the bloody birth throes of the new society can be shortened, simplified and concentrated: revolutionary terror," said Marx ("The Victory of the Counter-Revolution in Vienna," Neue Rheinische Zeitung, No. 136, November 1848). Marx inspired the socialists Stalin, Mao, and Hitler. Stalin and Hitler worked together. Stalin and Mao worked together.

Socialists, as their name declares, hate individualists; socialism opposes individualism. Socialists want everyone to be "equal" and they use force to make it happen, even if they have to kill people who socialists think are not willing or able to be "equal."

It is important to remember all of the deaths in the socialist Wholecaust (of which the Holocaust was a part) under Stalin, Mao, and Hitler (and others). That is something that Snyder does not want to talk about directly.

Snyder's book fails to analyze "socialism" as the political philosophy of both Hitler and Stalin, and the similarities and differences between how they used the word in their speeches and writings. His lectures perpetuate this shortcoming.

No historian can earn a grade of "A+" if his descriptions of Hitler and Stalin (and Mao et cetera) do not include their political philosophy of "socialism" and how they touted the word as their ideology. It is a question of intellectual dishonesty.

Snyder claims that Ayn Rand (Alisa Rosenbaum), who fled Soviet socialism, believed that competition was the meaning of life itself. Snyder claims that the socialist Hitler said "much the same thing" (?). Such reductionism by Snyder, although temptingly elegant, is fatal. It was fatal to millions under the socialists Hitler, Stalin, Mao, et cetera. Snyder did not reveal what Stalin and Mao said about competition. Snyder hides how Stalin, Mao, and Hitler droned on glowingly about "socialism" by the very word, and Rand did the opposite. Rand debunked them, just as her work debunks Snyder.

The socialists Hitler, Stalin, Mao and all socialists believe that competition is bad, and thus capitalism is bad, and both must be eliminated. Socialists who believe that Jews are capitalists want to eliminate Jews. Socialists eliminate Jews either by killing them or by banning their religion (e.g. Stalin, Mao, and Hitler).

Snyder is brainwashed with the absurd left/right political spectrum that is taught in government schools (socialist schools).

Snyder falls for the current fad of all socialists: climate change. "A problem that is truly planetary in scale, such as climate change, obviously demands global solutions -and one apparent solution is to define a global enemy" (Black Earth, page 327). Snyder suggests the same enemy (capitalists) who were named by the socialists Stalin, Mao, Hitler, and every other socialist, including all socialists today.

Socialists believe there is a pie of goods and everyone must fight for those goods by taking them from others. They dress up their violence and theft with the terms "taxation," and "socialism," and "for the good of all." That old socialist lie works well with "climate change," where the pie becomes the entire planet.

109

In his ecological panic, Snyder discusses China, comparing its current behavior to that of Germany under Hitler. It is painful (intellectually dishonest?) how Snyder evades any mention of the love of the word "socialism" by China's government and Germany's government (under Hitler). It reveals more about Snyder than it does about Chinese socialism and German socialism.

Snyder is everything he accuses others of being. Similar to socialist dictators, Snyder knows all about "climate change" and how to use socialism to force the "fix" on everyone. This is his trite insight: "We" have to "do something" about "insert current excuse here - CLIMATE CHANGE" (when what he really means is he wants to impose massive government intervention).

Snyder's climate change cliche' is a sad reminder of the old socialist excuse for millions who starved to death: "bad weather." What about the "environmental change" suffered under Stalin, Mao, Hitler, et cetera? Now the old socialist excuse for killing millions has been updated: "bad weather caused by capitalism." Snyder's solution: we don't have enough socialism yet.

Snyder uses "climate change" the same way other socialists do: it is a synonym for "capitalism." Snyder wants to stop climate change (capitalism). That is what all socialists want to do. Hitler said much the same thing. The difference is that Hitler actually used the word "socialism." All the time.

Which one impoverishes, enslaves, robs, tortures, and kills more people: socialism or "climate change" (capitalism)?

Snyder never blames socialism for his "climate change" facade. He does not fault socialism for socialized roads and for the interstate highway system where the U.S. government used military-socialism as its tardy excuse for following the socialist Hitler and his Autobahn. Snyder's response would be the stale socialist whine "But who will build the roads?!?!?!"

Snyder never blames all the socialist monopolies created and imposed by socialists: socialism's history of electricity monopolies, phone monopolies, road monopolies, utility monopolies. His silence indicates that he thinks socialist monopolies are grand and all fault lies elsewhere.

Similar to socialists, Snyder repeats the vague myth of the "business cycle." He has no comment on the "socialism cycle" that holds all the worst world records for mass slaughter. What is Snyder's prescription for the "socialism cycle"? Which one impoverishes, enslaves, robs, tortures, and kills more people: his undefined "business cycle" or the "socialism cycle"?

Socialists have been big winners of Darwin Awards: the recognition given to those "who improve our gene pool by removing themselves from it in a spectacularly stupid manner." The Union of Soviet Socialist Republics was one of the early winners of the "Honor" in 1917. Darwin Awards are given to those who perish through some "astonishing misapplications of judgment." Darwin Awards go hand-in-hand with the Big Whopper Liar's Contest (as if they were meshed S-letters for "socialism" in the swastika). Stalin, Mao, and Hitler were repeat recipients year after year for a long time.

Socialism spread to Germany, Russia and elsewhere with

111

help from the American socialists Francis and Edward Bellamy. An obituary for Edward Bellamy states: "It is stated that Emperor William purchased 1,000 copies of 'Looking Backward,' which he distributed among the students and working classes of Germany." (obituary dateline Springfield, Mass., May 22, 1898, "The Author of 'Looking Backward' has Passed Away").

Socialism spread from Francis Bellamy at the World's Fair from May 1893 to October 30, 1893, in Chicago. At that fair, the German firm Krupp had a pavilion of artillery (which cost approximately one million dollars).

In January 1892, in preparation for the World's Columbian Fair, the Youth's Companion magazine assigned Francis Bellamy to be manager for the National Public School Celebration of Columbus Day on October 11, 1892.

Columbus Day commemorates the explorer Christopher Columbus in a country named after Amerigo Vespucci, who exposed Columbus' mistaken belief that Columbus had visited Asia or India. In 1492, Native Americans discovered Columbus lost at sea. The country had been previously "discovered" by Leif Erikson and plenty of others, including the aborigines (the 1925 film "The Vanishing American" shows Native Americans being taught the Nazi salute and Bellamy's robotic chanting in a government school).

The Columbus Day holiday inspired Bellamy to write his "Address for Columbus Day" entitled "The Meaning of the Four Centuries," which was part of the program that included the pledge for the Youth's Companion Magazine. Bellamy was

112

hired by James B. Upham's uncle-by-marriage, Daniel S. Ford, to work for the popular magazine where Upham already worked. Upham and Bellamy collaborated to write the pledge.

Upham and Ford were aware of Francis Bellamy's Christian Socialist dogma before Bellamy was hired. Bellamy was a vice president of the Christian Society of Socialists. Bellamy was involved in so much radicalism and subversion that he was forced out of the ministry of his Boston church for his socialist sermons, including topics like "Jesus the Socialist."

The Pledge of Allegiance was a small part of a much larger program (authored and/or supervised by Bellamy) in the Youth's Companion magazine. The larger program included a reference to Rome. The program also included hymns, prayers, and various references to the Bible and God (including the phrase "under God") and more to tie socialism to the cross and Christianity. It was socialism as a religion.

Prayers, hymns and references to God have never ended in government (socialist) schools, because they are now the Pledge of Allegiance.

It is hard to believe that some people object to the Pledge of Allegiance only on the grounds of the two-word deification (added in 1954). Some argue falsely that Bellamy would have objected to the phrase and imply that Bellamy was an atheist. People who object only to the two-word deification "under God" are strange and fail to see the forest because they are staring at a single tree.

Bellamy's dogma was the same argument used later by

113

German Christians under Hitler's socialism and under Germany's hooked cross (see Gerhard Hahn, Christuskreuz und Hakenkreuz, Schriftenreihe der "Deutschen Christen" Hannovers, Nr. 1 (1934)). In the German churches, the Christian Cross was next to the Hooked Cross. In American churches, the Christian Cross was (and is) next to the U.S. flag, whose pledge was the origin of the Nazi salute, and whose mechanical chanting continues today.

Another ominous parallel between the German socialist Adolf Hitler and the American socialist Francis Bellamy is that they were both doing what socialists do: using government to make money. The worst form of greed and selfishness is not capitalism, it is socialism. Bellamy promoted government schools (socialist schools) in order to sell flags; Hitler was using government to sell his un-sellable book. China's Mao was similar with his "little red book."

The eerie part is that Bellamy's scheme has not stopped. It seems impossible to know how much money the government spends to put U.S. flags (made in China) in government (socialist) schools for the ritual that spawned the Nazi salute and Nazi behavior.

An even bigger number is the outrageous amount of stolen money the government takes to monopolize education. That is another ominous parallel between German socialism and American socialism.

Bellamy's plan to spread his dogma globally was boosted when Bellamy became chairman of a committee to form a World Congress of Youth at the Columbia Exposition in

Chicago in 1893. The World's Youth Congress Auxiliary (or World Congress Auxiliary) asked The Youth's Companion magazine (where Francis Bellamy worked) to organize the scheme. A. F. Nightingale was president of the Youth's World Congress. More details are provided in a newspaper article, "Youths at the World's Fair," from the Daily Gleaner on August 22, 1892 ("The Gleaner" continues to publish in Jamaica and states that it was established in 1834). The article explains that the congress would be composed of youths of all nations of the World (and many countries are listed including Germany, Russia, Italy, France and "countries of the Orient"). The youths will "stand before the generation to follow us as witnesses of the humanizing power of the World's Exposition of 1893, and be inspired by its influence to higher and more useful careers, making the fulfillment of its great promises their noblest claim to history." The "humanizing power" that Bellamy brought to the World's Exposition of 1893 (and the fulfillment of Bellamy's "noblest" claim to history) was the Nazi salute and robotic chanting to flags daily in military formation in government schools (socialist schools).

The "Brotherhood of man" cliché that is used in the newspaper article was a popular cliché with the international Theosophical Society, which promoted the dogma of Francis Bellamy and Edward Bellamy. The Theosophical Society also utilized the swastika symbol to promote its socialist dogma.

Bellamy's international aspiration for his World Youth Congress is one of the reasons why Bellamy's original pledge did not reference the "flag of the United States of America."

Bellamy wrote his pledge so that it could be adopted by other countries. He wanted to spread military socialism worldwide.

Did those "coming leaders of mankind" from the World Youth Congress include people who became supporters of the socialists Stalin, Mao, and Hitler?

10. HITLER'S SOCIALIST MEIN KAMPF

The following is a list of words that shed light on the police state touted by the socialist Hitler in Mein Kampf. Much can be learned from how often some words were used, or whether specific words were used at all (some of the listed words are followed by comments, and their frequency of use may or may not be noted. The information is also impacted by which translation of Mein Kampf is searched). This review is preliminary:

Armlet: 5 times? (Hitler explained that his notorious red armbands were learned from Marxists: "In Berlin, after the War, I was present at a mass-demonstration of Marxists in front of the Royal Palace and in the Lustgarten. A sea of red flags, red armlets and red flowers was in itself sufficient to give that huge assembly of about 120,000 persons an outward appearance of strength. I was now able to feel and understand how easily the man in the street succumbs to the hypnotic magic of such a grandiose piece of theatrical presentation"). Pledging Allegiance to flags is another example of such hypnosis.

Aryan: used 58 times? (Hitler's concept of the "super socialist man"). See more on the use of the term "Aryan" near the end of this chapter.

Blood: ?

Bourgeois: used 191 times?

Bolshevic, Bolshevization, Bolshevism, or Bolshevized, etc. Used 27 times? ("To-day Germany is the next battlefield for Russian Bolshevism").

Chinaman: ?

Christian-Socialist: 15 times? (and Christian-Socialist Party).

Communist: "For the National Socialist Movement has set itself to the task of converting those communists."

Eisner: ? (and Kurt Eisner)

Fascist: appears once as a reference to Italy?

Heil: 4 times? (Hitler mentions hearing "HEIL HOHENZOLLERN" shouted in Vienna). The notorious stiff-armed gesture that German socialists adopted later is not specifically mentioned in Mein Kampf.

Left: 5? In the sense of "left" wing.

Marx, Marxist: ?

Movement 596?

The Movement 193?

Nazi, Nazis, Nazism: does not appear.

Nigger: 3 times?

Pan-German: 44 times? (and "Pan-German Party" or "Pan-German Movement").

Racial 136?

Racialist, race-based: ?

Red: ?

Reich: ? (but no mention of the phrase "Third Reich").

Right: 1 time? In the sense of "right" wing?

Roman: ?

Sieg: ?

Siegfried: ?

Slav: 4?; Slavs: 8?; Slavic: 16?;

slave: 4?; slaves: 10?; slavery: 8?; enslave: 2? Hitler does not comment about the etymology relationship (in German and English) of the terms for "Slav" and "slave." Hitler seems ignorant of that the word "Caucasus" as it relates to the word "Caucasian," in that the word "slave" originated from Caucasians and other Slavs who were enslaved).

Storm Detachment: 25?

Swastika: does not appear in the original German language (where "Hakenkreuz" was used), but is always used in translations, and without any explanation of the choice of "swastika" over "hooked cross." The term "Hakenkreuz" translates almost literally as "hook cross" (or "hooked cross") and avoids the confusion caused by translation to "swastika."

Vienna: 80 times?

Weltanschauung: used 84 times? Sometimes translated as "race-based society"?

There are popular misconceptions about Hitler's use of the term "Aryan." This section of this chapter examines the use of the term "Aryan" in Mein Kampf. The following analyzes the 1939 Murphy version of Mein Kampf.

....

The following example indicates Hitler is using the term "Aryan" to refer to more than one set of people.

(p 228) "Aryan tribes, often almost ridiculously small in number, subjugated foreign peoples and, stimulated by the conditions of life which their new country offered them (fertility, the nature of the climate, etc.), and profiting also by the abundance of manual labour furnished them by the inferior race, they developed intellectual and organizing faculties which had hitherto been dormant in these conquering tribes."

....

(page 226)? "Within a few decades the whole of Eastern Asia, for instance, appropriated a culture and called such a culture its own, whereas the basis of that culture was the Greek mind and Teutonic skill as we know it. Only the external form - at least to a certain degree - shows the traits of an Asiatic inspiration. It is not true, as some believe, that Japan adds European technique to a culture of her own. The truth rather is that European science and technics are just decked out with the peculiar characteristics of Japanese civilization. The

121

foundations of actual life in Japan to-day are not those of the native Japanese culture, although this characterizes the external features of the country, which features strike the eye of European observers on account of their fundamental difference from us; but the real foundations of contemporary Japanese life are the enormous scientific and technical achievements of Europe and America, that is to say, of Aryan peoples. Only by adopting these achievements as the foundations of their own progress can the various nations of the Orient take a place in contemporary world progress. The scientific and technical achievements of Europe and America provide the basis on which the struggle for daily livelihood is carried on in the Orient. They provide the necessary arms and instruments for this struggle, and only the outer forms of these instruments have become gradually adapted to Japanese ways of life.

If, from to-day onwards, the Aryan influence on Japan would cease - and if we suppose that Europe and America would collapse - then the present progress of Japan in science and technique might still last for a short duration; but within a few decades the inspiration would dry up, and native Japanese character would triumph, while the present civilization would become fossilized and fall back into the sleep from which it was aroused about seventy years ago by the impact of Aryan culture."

....

(p 231) "The Aryan neglected to maintain his own racial stock unmixed and therewith lost the right to live in the paradise which he himself had created. He became submerged in the racial mixture and gradually lost his cultural creativeness, until he finally grew, not only mentally but also physically, more like the aborigines whom he had subjected rather than his own ancestors. For some time he could continue to live on the capital of that culture which still remained; but a condition of fossilization soon set in and he sank into oblivion. That is how cultures and empires decline and yield their places to new formations."

....

(p 232) "The readiness to sacrifice one's personal work and, if necessary, even one's life for others shows its most highly developed form in the Aryan race. The greatness of the Aryan is not based on his intellectual powers, but rather on his willingness to devote all his faculties to the service of the community. Here the instinct for self-preservation has reached its noblest form; for the Aryan willingly subordinates his own ego to the common weal and when necessity calls he will even sacrifice his own life for the community."

....

(p 234) "The Jew offers the most striking contrast to the Aryan."

....

(p 237) "We ought to remember that during the first period of American colonization numerous Aryans earned their daily livelihood as trappers and hunters, etc., frequently wandering about in large groups with their women and children, their mode of existence very much resembling that of ordinary nomads. The moment, however, that they grew more numerous and were able to accumulate larger resources, they cleared the land and drove out the aborigines, at the same time establishing settlements which rapidly increased all over the country."

....

(p 239) "In the Aryan mind no religion can ever be imagined unless it embodies the conviction that life in some form or other will continue after death."

....

(p 241) "A development began which has always been the same or similar wherever and whenever Jews came into contact with Aryan peoples."

....

(p 241) here the term "Aryan" appears to be used simply as a synonym for "non-Jew."

"[The Jew's] commercial cunning, acquired through thousands of years of negotiation as an intermediary, made him superior in this field to the Aryans, who were still quite ingenuous and indeed clumsy and whose honesty was unlimited; so that after a short while commerce seemed destined to become a Jewish monopoly."

....

(p 276) "Those who effectively combat this mortal enemy of our people, who is at the same time the enemy of all Aryan peoples and all culture, can only expect to arouse opposition on the part of this race and become the object of its slanderous attacks. "

....

(p 332) "One thing is certain: our world is facing a great revolution. The only question is whether the outcome will be propitious for the Aryan portion of mankind or whether the everlasting Jew will profit by it.

By educating the young generation along the right lines, the People's State will have to see to it that a generation of mankind is formed which will be adequate to this supreme combat that will decide the destinies of the world.

That nation will conquer which will be the first to take this road."

....

(p 346) "The constructive principle of Aryan humanity is thus displaced by the destructive principle of the Jews, They become the 'ferment of decomposition' among nations and races and, in a broad sense, the wreckers of human civilization."

....

(p 351) "Any party that is led by him can fight for no other interests than his, and his interests certainly have nothing in common with those of the Aryan nations."

....

(p 384) "We National Socialists regarded our flag as being the embodiment of our party programme. The red expressed the social thought underlying the movement. White the national thought. And the swastika signified the mission allotted to us - the struggle for the victory of Aryan mankind and at the same time the triumph of the ideal of creative work which is in itself and always will be anti-Semitic."

....

(p 429) "Catholics and Protestants are fighting with one another to their hearts' content, while the enemy of Aryan humanity and all Christendom is laughing up his sleeve."

....

(p 429) "This pestilential adulteration of the blood, of which hundreds of thousands of our people take no account, is being systematically practised by the Jew to-day. Systematically these negroid parasites in our national body corrupt our innocent fair-haired girls and thus destroy something which can no longer be replaced in this world."

....

(p 429) "For the future of the world, however, it does not matter which of the two triumphs over the other, the Catholic or the Protestant. But it does matter whether Aryan humanity survives or perishes. And yet the two Christian denominations are not contending against the destroyer of Aryan humanity but are trying to destroy one another."

....

(p 489) "In place of preaching hatred against Aryans from whom we may be separated on almost every other ground but with whom the bond of kindred blood and the main features of a common civilization unite us, we must devote ourselves to arousing general indignation against the maleficent enemy of humanity and the real author of all our sufferings."

....

(p 495) "They would remain as the fertilizing manure of civilization, until the last residue of Nordic-Aryan blood would

126

become corrupted or drained out."

....

(p 309) "A benefit which results from the fact that there was no all-round assimilation is to be seen in that even now we have large groups of German Nordic people within our national organization, and that their blood has not been mixed with the blood of other races. We must look upon this as our most valuable treasure for the sake of the future."

11. SIGNS & SIGNATURES OF SOCIALISM

Hitler changed the Hakenkreuz, and Hitler changed his own signature in a similar way. Rarely seen autographs from Hitler show that he evolved his signature "Adolf Hitler" into "S Hitler." It was a declaration of his socialism every time he signed his name: as if he was signing "Socialist Hitler."

Most people have never seen Hitler's signature. That is because the media never display Hitler's signature and do not want readers to know what it reveals.

Ernst "Putzi" Hanfstaengl (an intimate of Hitler's), also signed his name with a similar "swastika" flourish. Hanfstaengl, educated in the U.S., might have encouraged Hitler to adopt the American Nazi salute, as well as the "swastika" style signature.

There are signatures from other Hitler underlings that appear to use a "swastika" style flourish.

German military medals were cast with raised lettering that displays Hitler's "S" style signature.

In 1920, Hitler decided that the National Socialist German Workers' Party needed its own insignia. The new flag had to be "a symbol of our own struggle" as well as "highly effective as a poster." (Mein Kampf, Chapter 7 of the 2nd volume, sometimes pg. 495).

In Mein Kampf, Hitler described the new flag: "In red we see the social idea of the movement, in white the nationalistic idea, in the swastika the mission of the struggle for the victory of the Aryan man, and, by the same token, the victory of the idea of creative work..." (pg. 496-497).

In German the quoted reference was: "im Hakenkreuz die Mission des Kampfes fÜr den Sieg des arischen Menschen und zugleich mit ihm auch den Sieg des Gedankens der schaffenden Arbeit,"

In his own words, Hitler used the word "sieg" twice and can be interpreted as stating that the swastika is a "sieg" symbol. Also known as "sig runes," the "lightning-bolt" symbols are letters of an ancient Germanic alphabet. An internet image search for "double sig rune," "sig rune," "sieg rune," "sigel rune," or "sowilo" provides more examples. The "sieg" rune corresponds with the letter "S" and was used for "S" in other symbolism.

Hitler's quote has overlapping use of the word "sieg." The word "sieg" means "victory." His symbol represented two "S" letters for "socialism" or "socialism and sieg" (socialism and victory) and is related to "Sieg Heil!" (Hail to Victory) in the sense of "Hail to the Victory of Socialism!" (Hail to the Victory of the National Socialist German Workers' Party).

Hitler's quote refers to the red color and the "social idea of the movement" that ties into socialism for which Hitler claimed the National Socialist German Workers' Party was struggling for victory.

The struggle for victory began in 1919, when Hitler joined the German Workers' Party, a socialist group. The group sought a new name that would attract socialists in other groups. Other German socialist groups used terms like "National" and "Socialist" in their titles, and the German Workers' Party adopted "National Socialist German Workers' Party."

Hitler gave the Hakenkreuz symbol the same meaning as the group's new name. For Hitler, the joined "S" letters symbolized socialists joining together as the National Socialist German Workers' Party. The intertwined letter "S" shapes represent "Socialists" unified, or "Socialist Solidarity" and the victory of the National Socialist German Workers' Party bringing socialists together in one large group.

Hitler also wrote: "Two years later, when our squad of hall guards had long since grown into storm detachments, it seemed necessary to give this defensive organization of a young Weltanschhauung a particular symbol of victory, namely a Standard." In German it was: "Zwei Jahre spÄter, als aus der Ordnertruppe schon lÄngst eine viel tausend Mann umfassende Sturmabteilung geworden war, schien es nÖtig, dieser Wehrorganisation der jungen Weltanschauung noch ein besonderes Symbol des Sieges zu geben: die Standarte." Hitler again used the phrase "Symbol des Sieges." In the only comments on the symbol by Hitler, the Sturmabteilung was specifically referenced.

The Sturmabteilung had well-known Nazi banners that included Hitler's Hakenkreuz-swastika in the old style (horizontal / square), the new style (slanted / diamond), and another banner also utilizing another stylized "S" symbol, for the "SA" (Sturm Abteilung).

Hitler mentions "Siegfried" in Mein Kampf. Siegfried is a German language male given name, composed from the Germanic elements sig "victory" and frithu "protection, peace." The name is medieval, and survived into modern times and, after 1876, it enjoyed renewed popularity due to Richard Wagner's "Siegfried," the third of the four operas that constitute Der Ring des Nibelungen (The Ring of the Nibelung), inspired by the story of Sigurd in Norse mythology.

The term "Nazi" was (and is) a term of derision used by people against the National Socialists German Workers' Party. Party members did not use the term "Nazi" to refer to themselves. Party members used the terms "socialist" or "national socialist" or the full name of the party.

In the notorious 1934 film "Triumph of the Will" by Leni Riefenstahl, and in the 1925 book "Mein Kampf" by Adolf Hitler, the word "socialist" is used throughout and the words "Nazi" and "Fascist" are never used -not a single time- in reference to the National Socialist German Workers' Party. In the film, they refer to each other as "Kamerads" (comrades).

131

Stylized "S" letters were used in other symbolism under German National Socialists including Hitler's "SS" Division which used two similarly stylized "S" letters side-by-side for "Schutzstaffel," as compared with the overlapping "S" shapes of the Hakenkreuz / swastika;

Alphabetic lettering in a stylized form is shown in other Nazi-Sozi paraphernalia, in Nazi posters, in German medals, flags, banners, and including but not limited to the symbols of the "NSV" (National Socialist Volkswohlfahrt), and the "T-O" logo of the Todt Organization; and the Technische Nothilfe (abbreviated as TN, TeNo, TENO; literally: Technical Emergency Help).

Swastika-style symbolism is visible today and every day on the streets as the VW logo. The logo is two identical "V" letters crossed to form the letters "V" and "W" (or a "V" and a "W" letter joined) in a similar "hooked cross" alphabetical style for "Volkswagen." The VW was Hitler's socialist "People's Car" scam that he never produced for "the people" (because he was busy killing them in war).

Franz Xaver Reimspiess, Nikolai Borg, and others have claimed credit for the VW logo. Borg, a young commercial artist impressed others when he won the competition for the creation of a logo for the "Deutsche Jugendherbergswerk." Borg said that he was invited to draw the Volkswagen car logo in a request from high-up: Dr. Ing. Fritz Todt, with the "Organization Todt" the general inspector for roads and a militarily organized building troop used in the entire theater of war (boasting its own alphabetical symbol in the conjoined

132

letters "O" and "T" for its logo). Borg stated that he made nine drafts with different connections of the crossed "V" letters, to represent the letters "V" and "W" before his final version emerged. Borg has exhibited photographs in which Borg's VW emblem design was placed on top of the swastika symbol that inspired it, and was created simply by replacing the two crossed "S" letters of the swastika with the two crossed "V" letters (that also form the letters V and W).

Before the VW emblem was created, the symbol for Volkswagen was a swastika encircled by a cogwheel. It was the symbol for the organization that controlled Volkswagen, the socialist trade union organization Deutsche Arbeitsfront (DAF or German Labor Front). The swastika of the Deutsche Arbeitsfront emblem was the origin of the Volkswagen logo, both philosophically and stylistically.

Similar stylized symbolism is visible in the meshed "M" letters in the emblem of the Maybach automobile (from Maybach-Motorenbau); and the "S" shaped logo used with the Trabant Sachsenring car from Automobilwerke Zwickau (which also used a revealing "A-Z" logo). Audi's emblem evolved from four car companies that showed similar alphabetical symbolism in some early emblems.

A 1935 Youth's booklet from the National Socialist German Workers' Party shows that youngsters were taught about the "S" shapes of German socialist symbols. The entire 35-page book was uncovered by the symbologist Dr. Curry and it is the only example known to exist. Although the book is in its original German language, the illustrations supplement the text's explanation that common symbols under the National Socialist German Workers' Party often used the "S" shape, including the side-by-side use in the "SS" Division (for "Schutzstaffel") and the overlapping use in the Swastika.

This is a translation of excerpted text in the 1935 Nazi youth's book:

"Today, we are proud of our Germanic heritage; we wish German custom to again be in the lead over everything foreign, and to demonstrate this, the Hitler Youth has taken the old victory sign, the Siegrune, for their flags and armbands.

From the Siegrune "S" one can easily create an "S" "S" form [illustrations showed a stylized rune "S" next to an English-style alphabetic "S" letter]. And the Leader's Schutz-Staffel, which we abbreviate "SS", carries the double-rune "SS" [an illustration showed the classic stylized rune "SS"] as their badge. This victory and salvation rune may also be found in a stretched version, which looks like this [an illustration showed a longer version oriented horizontally]. Many bear a small line in the middle, [an illustration showed the previous version oriented horizontally and a short notch added in the middle] and is then known as Wolfsangel.

"I know something, I know something," Harmut suddenly explained, taking the pencil from his father's hand. "If you superimpose two Wolfsangels, you get a hooked-cross. This is also two Siegrunes." [an illustration showed a Hakenkreuz (swastika)]

"You have made a nice and meaningful discovery, my son," father happily noted, "because the....." [End of quote from that page of the 1935 Nazi youth book].

Each summer thousands of Hitler Youth marched from their hometowns down German roads to meet en masse at Nuremberg to join in the yearly rally and congress of the Nazi-socialists. The notorious film "Triumph of the Will" by Leni Riefenstahl from 1935 was propaganda for the sixth annual rally. The word "socialism" is used in a positive manner throughout the film by the speakers to extol their dogma. The words "Nazi" and "fascist" are never used in the film.

"Triumph of the Will" shows the National Socialist German Workers' Party parading its industrial army of military socialism. In keeping with their socialist dogma, Hitler is praised as an "epitome of altruism" and the speakers refer to each other as "comrades" who will cause a "revolution of the people and workers" to end "class struggle" and create "egalitarianism."

The following words were emphasized as shown in the book "Look to Germany" by Stanley McClatchie:

"NATIONAL SOCIALISM? What does it mean? The true significance of this name given to the German movement is usually overlooked, and the hasty reader at the breakfast table is prone to see - "National...ism".

THE GERMAN FLAG? What does it look like? The

majority of foreigners know that it contains a swastika and believe that this signifies only - "National...ism".

THE FLAG BEARERS? Who are they? The world regards their disciplined ranks, the brown uniforms and reflects - "National...ism".

It is time, however, to wake up!
S O C I A L I S M is the principle word in the title of the Movement. The basic colour in its banner is
 R E D and those who wear the brown uniforms are COMRADES!"

12. AMERICAN SOCIALISM IN ITALY

Benito Mussolini was a well-known and long-time socialist leader. Mussolini acquired his title "il duce" -leader- when he was known only as a socialist. As a socialist leader, he began to mimic American socialists in their use of the stiff-armed salute, robotic chanting to flags, the glorification of ancient Rome (or myths about Rome), and the use of the fasces symbol as an emblem of government and socialism.

In ancient Rome, the fasces [fas-eez] was a bundle of sticks bound together. It symbolized "union," or people banded together. Thus, the word "fascist" is related to the word "fagot" (or faggot (British)) as a bundle of wood (see the work of the etymologist Dr. Curry) and via the similar early pronunciation of the words "fasces" and "faggot" (the original Latin term "fasces" was pronounced with a hard letter "C" sound or /k/, not the modern soft letter "C" sound or /s/).

The concept extends to Greece and Aesop (believed to have lived in ancient Greece between 620 and 560 BCE). Fabulous research compares a translation from the Greek writing of one of Aesop's Fables known as "The Old Man and his Sons" or "The Bundle of Sticks." In the fable an old man on the point of death summoned his quarreling sons around him to give them some parting advice. He ordered his servants to bring in a faggot of sticks, and said to his eldest son: "Break it." The son strained and strained, but with all his efforts was unable to break the Bundle. The other sons also tried, but none of them was successful. "Untie the faggots," said the father, "and each of you take a stick." When they had done so, he called out to them: "Now, break," and each stick was easily broken. "You see my meaning," said their father. And the meaning was supposed to be: Union gives strength.

Mussolini's message was: Individually we are weak like a single twig, but in a bundle we are a mighty faggot.

In another bizarre parallel to "Christian Socialism," the phrase "fire and faggot" described punishment of a heretic by burning. Heretics who recanted were forced to display the symbol of a faggot on their shirt sleeve for public humiliation.

Homosexuality was illegal under the old crusades, under early "Christian socialism," and under the modern socialist crusades of the socialists Stalin, Mao, Hitler, Mussolini, Castro, Pol Pot, in North Korea, et cetera.

The derogatory term for a "male homosexual," 1914, is probably from the earlier use for an old heretical woman, and a reference to the "flaming faggots" (homosexuals were also burned at the stake).

"Heretics" under modern socialist Crusades might include Fanya Kaplan and Charlotte Corday.

The word "fasces" is also related to these words: fascine, fascia, fascinate, fasciatus fish, plantar fasciitis, and many more.

Fascism meant "unionism" to the socialist Benito Mussolini. Mussolini's socialist "unionism" mimicked "soviets" (councils) under Russian socialism (the Union of Soviet Socialist Republics). It was Mussolini's version of socialist syndicalism. Both the Italian and Soviet systems were similar to the organization that arose later under German socialism (the National Socialist German Workers Party).

On December 11, 1914, Mussolini started a political group: Fasci d'azione Rivoluzionaria (Union of Revolutionary Action). It combined two other movements: (1) Fasci d'azione Rivoluzionaria Internazionalista and (2) Fasci Autonomi d'azione Rivoluzionaria (a previous group he started).

"Fasci" referred to Mussolini's socialist union for socialist revolution. It is similar to the word "faction" in that Mussolini's group was another of many socialist-inspired unions.

The term "fascio" was the Italian word for workers' groups, peasant organizations, labor unions and the other socialist groups where Mussolini had developed a large following.

The Fasci d'azione Rivoluzionaria asserted that it supported socialism, using the famous quote by French socialist Louis Auguste Blanqui, "He who has iron has bread" on the title page of its socialist newspaper, Il Popolo d'Italia. The newspaper announced under its title that it was the "Socialist Daily" (Quotidiano Socialista).

After some indecision, Mussolini supported World War I by appealing to the need for socialists to overthrow the Hohenzollern and Habsburg monarchies in Germany and Austria-Hungary. Mussolini claimed that they had consistently repressed socialism. Mussolini argued that hundreds of thousands of Italians were under Habsburg rule. He asserted that the defeat of Hohenzollern and Habsburg monarchies would help the working class.

Mussolini explained that the war would bring Tsarist Russia to social revolution. He gleefully predicted and supported the socialist revolution that formed the Union of Soviet Socialist Republics (USSR).

In 1919, Mussolini created a new socialist sub-group called "Fasci di combattimento" (also known as the "Fascio nazionale di combattimento"). It referred to his socialist band of combat. It was another use of the word that is similar to "faction" to designate socialist-inspired unions. Socialism is always faction against faction. On 9 November 1921, Mussolini transformed the Fasci Italiani di Combattimento into the National Fascist Party.

Socialism then grew in Germany with the German Workers' Party (Deutsche Arbeiterpartei, DAP) and Hitler's membership therein. On February 24, 1920, Hitler decided to change the name of his group (the DAP). On that date, Mussolini continued to be known as a socialist leader in Italy (although he used the term "fasci" for some of his socialist union sub-groups), and Lenin continued to be known as a socialist leader in the Union of Soviet Socialist Republics. The DAP changed its name to the Nationalsozialistische Deutsche Arbeiterpartei (National Socialist German Workers Party). Hitler did not adopt Mussolini's use of the term "fasci" in any form. Hitler's socialists never self-identified as "Fascists," nor as "Nazis."

Benito Mussolini did NOT say: "Fascism should more appropriately be called Corporatism because it is a merger of State and corporate power." That fake quote was commonly attributed to Mussolini until the attribution was debunked by the veteran historian Dr. Rex Curry.

Some people point to Giovanni Gentile (in "La Dottrina del Fascismo") as the person who created the fake quote that was attributed to Mussolini. "La Dottrina del Fascismo" was written by Giovanni Gentile, and published under Mussolini's name in the Encyclopedia Italiana. However, the only reference to "corporatism" within Gentile's article is in section VIII, and NOT in the words of the quote.

There is no original source in Italian that refers to the quotation. Instead, there is one source in Italian, that translates an American source.

Mussolini never uttered the quote that is attributed to him, and anyone who understands what Mussolini DID say would know that the quote does not describe Mussolini's beliefs.

On July 2, 1926, Mussolini established the Ministry of Corporations and soon thereafter the National Council of Corporations. The wacky Italian socialists also created the

141

Istituto per la Ricostruzione Industriale (IRI). They were ominous parallels to Lenin's Soviet socialism at that time, and what would happen later under Hitler's German socialism, and Roosevelt's American socialism.

Mussolini's Ministry of Corporations organized the Italian economy into 22 "sectoral corporations" (see the Address to the National Corporative Council on November 14, 1933, and the Senate Speech on the Bill Establishing the Corporations on January 13, 1934). The 22 sectoral corporations were the method via which the socialist Mussolini organized his Unionism (Fascism), and his beloved worker's unions, and the economy. It was not until February 5, 1934, that the 22 "corporations" were defined:

1. Social Care & Credit
2. Internal Communications
3. Sea & Air
4. Entertainment
5. Hostelries
6. Professions & Arts
7. Building Construction
8. Water, Gas & Electricity
9. Mining Industries
10. Glass & Ceramics
11. Grains
12. Vegetable, Flower & Fruit Cultivation
13. Wine and Oil Cultivation
14. Livestock & Fish

15. Wood
16. Textiles
17. Clothing
18. Metalworking
19. Machinery
20. Chemicals
21. Liquid Combustibles & Fossil Fuels
22. Paper & Publishing

They were not capitalist "corporations" as is claimed by some socialists in the USA. Socialists deliberately lie about what the socialist Mussolini was saying. Socialists misuse Mussolini's term. Mussolini's "corporations" defeated free markets, businesses, industry, and capitalism.

Mussolini didn't mean the power of big corporations. He meant the power of a large number of individuals working collectively as a bureaucracy or union. That is what he meant by "corporativismo."

Mussolini's term is closer to the concept of a municipal corporation, which is a form of socialism: a government entity that imposes a socialist monopoly on the provision of goods and services.

Socialists say they want to end "corporations" until they are asked, "You want to end municipal corporations?" After socialists research the meaning of "municipal corporation" they admit that they support the worst form of corporations (municipal corporations), and they share so much with the socialist Mussolini.

143

Mussolini's doppelganger in the United States was Franklin Delano Roosevelt (FDR). The twin-brothers suckled like wolves on the public teat, competed to be degenerate statists, raced to create new bureaucracies, and spread the roaming mythology of socialism. FDR grew up doing the stiff-armed socialist salute (during the Pledge of Allegiance and also outside of the pledge) long before the socialist leader Mussolini learned it. FDR was merely one in a long line of presidents and other famous Americans who helped teach the notorious gesture to Italy and the world.

Each one of Mussolini's socialist bureaucracies has one or more extant twins among the thousands of alphabet agencies in the United States (and many predate and influenced Mussolini's socialism) including: the Department of Agriculture (USDA 1862); Department of Commerce (1903, 1913); Department of Labor (1903, 1913); Department of the Interior (1849); Social Security Administration; Federal Communications Commission; Department of Health and Human Services; United States Postal Service; Bureau of Land Management; Department of Transportation; Federal Trade Commission; Federal Aviation Administration.

13. USA'S AUGUST LANDMESSER

August Landmesser is best known for his appearance in a photograph wherein he refused to perform the stiff-armed salute under German socialism during the launch of a naval training vessel (the Horst Wessel) on 13 June 1936.

No article about Landmesser points out that the same gesture (and persecution of anyone who refused the gesture) was happening in the United States at the same time that it was happening in Germany to Landmesser and others; that the Pledge of Allegiance to the U.S. flag was the origin of the gesture that Landmesser defied. Only in the comments section do people reference the work of Dr. Curry showing that the U.S. was the origin of the Nazi salute and Nazi behavior from the American socialist Francis Bellamy.

No article about Landmesser points out that the same behavior continues in the USA, where only the gesture has changed. Everyday in government schools (socialist schools) children robotically chant in unison on command. The gesture changed to hide the pledge's putrid past. Children are kept ignorant of the history of the quotidian ritual that they are led to perform.

No article about Landmesser explains that a growing wave of students refuse to be bullied into the brainwashing, and are learning the truth about the Pledge's putrid past. No one celebrates their bravery. Such students attract criticism in the media, and even dead silence from people who praise August Landmesser and who have nothing to say about the fact that Americans were persecuted (at the same time that Landmesser was persecuted in Germany) for refusing to perform the nazi salute in the Pledge of Allegiance in the USA.

No article about Landmesser includes photos of Americans circa 1936 that are very similar to the Landmesser photo. Has anyone in the media printed such a photo, or do any of them even have that knowledge?

There are court cases involving prison for Americans who refused to do the Nazi salute for the USA's pledge or who otherwise showed "disrespect" to the U.S. flag. Americans were beaten, imprisoned, even lynched.

The government and government schools deserve blame for that photo of Landmesser. Francis Bellamy deserves blame for Landmesser's predicament.

The photo of Landmesser is powerful and would be more powerful if Americans were not so ignorant of the history of the Pledge of Allegiance as the origin of the Nazi salute and Nazi behavior.

14. YESTERYEAR'S INDOCTRINATION

Francis Julius Bellamy died on August 28, 1931 in Tampa, Florida. Tampa was also the city where Bellamy's Pledge of Allegiance died. A plaque memorializes him and his pledge at the house where he resided on 2926 Wallcraft Avenue.

Although he died in Tampa, Bellamy's remains were moved to Rome, New York, the origin of the "ancient Roman salute" myth that developed from his pledge.

He lived long enough to see the government schools (socialist schools) that he wanted to impose on everyone. He lived long enough to see those schools impose segregation by law and teach racism as official policy, and force children to perform the Nazi salute and robotic chanting daily for 12 years of their lives, upon threat of violence or punishment. He lived through a time when people were beaten, arrested, jailed, imprisoned, and even lynched for defying his pledge.

No evidence has been found that any of the above bothered him, nor that he considered any of the above to be inconsistent with his dogma of "Christian socialism" and "Military socialism."

His work continues to haunt the world. The American Nazi salute continues to be used in many places, including Mexico, China (including Taiwan), and Russia.

Another subtitle for this book could be "To see or not see Nazi reality." The real "not sees" are people who do not see the socialist symbolism of the swastika and the Pledge of Allegiance. This book was written to educate modern "not-sees."

The cult of socialism was the same as the occult nightmares whispered about Nazism. The swastika was a symbol of "socialist" identity. The chosen people of the National Socialist German Workers' Party were a bizarre para-military fraternity that wanted to evolve and impose a new world order, creating a utopian future, similar to the Military Socialism and Christian Socialism of American socialists (including Francis Bellamy and Edward Bellamy).

Why does socialism inspire misanthropy, atrocities and mass slaughter?

People who adopted the "Double S" and its dogma of socialism preached the sacrifice of everyone. They called it a brave new world, but it was a grave new world.

The misanthropes, necrophiliacs and cannibals caused millions of deaths in the socialist Wholecaust (of which the Holocaust was a part): ~50 million under the Union of Soviet

148

Socialist Republics?; ~40 million under the Peoples' Republic of China?; ~20 million under the National Socialist German Workers' Party? Those eras are known as the modern socialist inquisitions, the modern socialist dark ages (and their inhumanity and death tolls exceeded that of the previous dark ages and of all prior inquisitions). It was the worst death toll in human history and so large that all Holocaust Museums could quadruple in size and scope by adding Wholecaust Museums to document the entire socialist slaughter.

Socialists fancied themselves as the "illuminati," but they were the "deluminati." Today, on world maps, they are the countries where the least light shines at night. Their psycho-pathology set and holds the worst records for extinguishing the life lights of so many.

The socialist psychopathy of the Bellamys continues in the USA today. Many Bellamy policies caused the oppressive domestic government. The pledge continues along with laws mandating that teachers lead the robotic intonation every day for twelve years in the life of each child.

The anti-libertarian government continues to own and operate schools, including the same schools that imposed segregation by law and taught racism as official government policy. The USA's practice of imposing segregation by law (in government schools) and teaching racism as official policy even outlasted the National Socialist German Workers Party into the 1960's and beyond.

After segregation in government schools ended, the Bellamy legacy caused more police-state racism of forced busing that destroyed communities and neighborhoods and deepened hostilities. Those schools still exist. Also extant are the same governmental bodies and their busing systems.

When a student enrolls, Government schools demand social security numbers (socialist slave numbers or "SS numbers") that were given to students as newborn infants to track and control them for life, stealing the whole way.

SS numbers were imposed in 1935, and many of the USA's slaves gleefully tattooed their numbers into their skin. That was years before tattooed numbers were used at Auschwitz under German socialism. SS number 535-07-5248 is tattooed on Thomas Cave in a 1939 photograph from Dorothea Lange.

Were there any instances of Americans burning their SS cards in protest?

Lange is also known for a photo of Japanese-American children saying the pledge of allegiance (with the hand-over-the heart) soon after President Franklin Delano Roosevelt ordered the relocation of 120,000 Japanese-Americans into internment camps. Lange's hand-over-the-heart pic should be compared with another photograph that shows Japanese-Americans performing the stiff-armed salute to the flag inside one of FDR's internment camps.

The hand-over-the-heart continues today in G-schools (government schools) where each classroom contains a Flag, and where small children are led in robotic chanting at the ring of a bell daily.

The school ritual led to flags in churches and temples. Flags in religious establishments also evolved from the "Christian

Socialism" and "Military Socialism" of Francis Bellamy and Edward Bellamy.

Inside a mosque, you will not find flags of ISIS, Al-Qaeda, or of terrorist organizations. In government schools, most Muslim students feel it is improper to pledge allegiance to the flag, nor to anything or anyone other than God.

In non-muslim churches and temples you will find the flag of the USA (and memorials to the government traveling around the world killing people).

Bellamy's pledge is different from the Bay`ah (Pledge of Allegiance) in Islam, where a Muslim pledges obedience to the ruler of a region. After the Pulse nightclub in Orlando was attacked in June of 2015, the government released transcripts of a 911 phone call with the culprit's "pledge of allegiance" that was censored so heavily that it was not clear whether or not the culprit pledged allegiance to the U.S. flag. The Muslim pledge is only recited once, whereas Bellamy's Bay`ah is recited by little children en masse and every day for 12 years as prescribed by state laws.

The pledge continues as enforced infantilism; adult simpletons chant the anachronistic childish Nazi artifact that was written more than a century ago for kindergartners.

How did so many people over the decades write about the USA's Pledge of Allegiance and the swastika and fail to make the discoveries in this book (discoveries that were made by Dr. Curry)? What caused the forgotten history? How could those writers (some of whom viewed historic photographs of the early pledge's Nazi salute), have failed (or refused?) to even ask the questions: (1) Was the Pledge of Allegiance the origin of the Nazi salute and Nazi behavior? (2) Did it impact Germany and other countries at all?

The societal amnesia is the fault of government's schools (socialist schools) that will never ask these questions about the daily pledge ritual and its relationship to socialism in Germany and worldwide. The government's schools have conditioned researchers and writers not to ask or answer the questions that have been answered here.

The word "Nazi" is used to hide the true origin of "Nazi": it means "national socialist." The word "Nazi" evolved from the first two syllables of the German word "national" in the term "national socialist." Hitler did not call himself a "Nazi"; he called himself a "national socialist." Bellamy did not call himself a "Nazi"; he called himself a "national socialist." The word "Nazi" continues to be used to cover up the connections between German socialism and American socialism. Francis Bellamy was a Nazi; he was an American Nazi.

Those are some of the reasons why government schools are unconstitutional: they violate the First Amendment right to freedom of speech and freedom of the press. The government schools (socialist schools) tell everyone what to think and say and write.

The Pledge of Allegiance is a fundamental part of the USA's police state. The pledge is a daily Milgram experiment, a witch hunt, and it demonstrates the banality of evil. Litigation continues to occur for persecution of people who refuse.

152

Fight antidisestablishmentarianism. Please help stop the Pledge of Allegiance and the socialism that it promotes and perpetuates. Remove the pledge from the flag, remove flags from schools, and remove schools from government.

Support the "Stop the Pledge of Allegiance Foundation." Take the pledge not to pledge.

15. BACKGROUND FOR THIS BOOK

The author Jonah Goldberg in the book "Liberal Fascism: The Secret History of the American Left, From Mussolini to the Politics of Meaning" cites Dr. Rex Curry. The following is an excerpt:

Religion was the glue that held this American national socialism together. Bellamy believed that his brand of socialist nationalism was the true application of Jesus' teachings. His cousin Francis Bellamy, the author of the Pledge of Allegiance, was similarly devoted. A founding member of the first Nationalist Club of Boston and co-founder of the Society of Christian Socialists, Francis wrote a Sermon, "Jesus, the Socialist," that electrified parishes across the country. In an expression of his "military socialism," the Pledge of Allegiance was accompanied by a

[stiff-arm] salute to the flag in American public schools. Indeed, some contend that the Nazis got the idea for their salute from America. (page 216).

...The story of the Pledge of Allegiance and its National Socialist roots is a fascinating one. Dr. Rex Curry, a passionate libertarian, has made the issue his white whale. (page 440, n. 25)

The book "From a 'Race of Masters' to a 'Master Race': 1948 to 1848" by the author A. E. Samaan (2013) states:

Dr. Rex Curry, the professor and attorney from Florida, has debated and largely proven the unavoidable evidence that Hitler's National Socialism was significantly influenced by Bellamy's 'nationalistic' form of 'socialism.' Curry is famous for making the claim that Hitler adopted the 'stiff-arm salute' from Francis and Edward Bellamy. (page 589).

Thus, Dr. Curry's claims that much of the fanfare and propaganda we now attribute to the Hitler Youth and the Nuremberg rallies actually originated with American customs, are definitely sound. (Samaan at page 590).

Professor Curry ... has been researching the link between Hitler's National Socialism and Edward Bellamy's 'socialistic' form of 'nationalism.' (Samaan at page 594).

The Sonoran News in Arizona explained the following in an article by Linda Bentley:

....**Dr. Rex Curry, a libertarian lawyer who has done vast research on the Pledge's socialist roots, provides pro bono services nationwide to educate students and teachers about 'the right to reject robotic ritualism.' The history of the Pledge simply proves Upham and Ford were able to capitalize on the promotion of Bellamy's socialist agenda, and it's not over yet.**

From the Daily Herald, in Provo, Utah, with Randy Wright, the Executive Editor:

Dear Dr. Curry -- Thanks for your help on short notice last night. The subject of the Pledge of Allegiance came up in connection with a rally at a local college in support of the phrase 'under God.' Your material made a terrific sidebar. Little known facts from the past.

From "God Save the South: A Treasure Chest of Forbidden Information," By John Thomas Nall:

The Pledge of Allegiance (1892) was the origin of the raised arm salute adopted later by the National Socialist

156

German Workers Party (Nazis). The Pledge was written by Francis Bellamy, cousin to Edward Bellamy (the author), and both were self-proclaimed national socialists in the United States. The original Pledge began with a military salute that was then extended out toward the flag. In practice, the second gesture was performed palm down. The gesture was not an ancient Roman salute. All of these are discoveries of the symbologist Dr. Rex Curry (author of "Pledge of Allegiance Secrets"). (page 208).

In "Cosmic Evolution: The Accelerated Human," the author James B Lawrence wrote:

...new discoveries show that American soldiers used the swastika as their symbol early in World War I, and up to 1941, against Germany. The symbol was used by Americans in the French Escadrille Lafayette, by the 45th Infantry Division, and on Boeing P-12 planes. The discoveries are in the growing body of work by the historian Dr. Rex Curry (author of 'Swastika Secrets'). He has previously shown how socialists in the USA originated the modern swastika as overlapping 'S' letters for 'Socialists' joining together in a utopian 'Socialist Society.' During the time when American soldiers adopted the swastika, the symbol was associated in the USA with the growing popularity of 'military socialism,' a dogma touted by Edward Bellamy, the American author of the international bestseller 'Looking Backward,' (1887) known as the bible of National Socialism. The symbol was also famous in the USA as alphabetical symbolism for socialism in the Theosophical Society (TS), from 1875. In 1888, the Theosophical Society teamed up with Bellamy's Nationalist movement for military socialism. The 'Bellamy swastika' spread. By 1915, the symbol was also widely popular as an ornamental 'Good Luck' symbol, as in a 1915 postcard showing the American flag posed favorably with a swastika. (Introduction page ix and in works cited).

Pastor Alvin H Franzmeier: "...the Sig-Rune became an 'S' and two together became the swastika and represented socialists joining together to form the National Socialist German Workers' party. In 1935 the swastika flag became official for Germany. The swastika symbol was not called that, but rather a HakenKreuz or hooked cross. This was Hitler's attempt to unite the church with the state, especially since German culture was strongly influenced by Christianity. You can find more on these topics on Rex Curry's website and its various pages. He has some interesting things to say about the use of the swastika also in America up to the start of WW II, as well as the open hand salute. The symbol was used by various socialist groups, not only in the USA, but also in the USSR."

Matt Crypto: "Before Dr. Curry's work, I had never viewed photographs nor film footage showing the early Nazi salute of the Pledge of Allegiance. At that time, I did

not even know that the Nazis were the 'National Socialist German Workers Party' and that they did not refer to themselves as 'Nazis.' I once doubted the greatness of His Excellency Professor Doctor Sir Rex Curry, but he sure put me in my place. Never flag in the fight for freedom!"

From Wikipedia: **"The American socialist Francis Bellamy's Pledge of Allegiance to the U.S. flag was the origin of the Nazi salute and Nazi behavior (e.g. robotic chanting to flags) under Hitler's German socialism. German socialists used the Nazi flag's symbol to represent crossed 'S' letters for their socialism (see work of the historian Dr. Rex Curry)."**

Jimmy Wales, Wikipedia's founder, has also commented on the influence of Dr. Curry's work on Wikipedia. The discoveries have been publicized and verified by many readers and writers on Wikipedia.

It is unfortunate that Wikipedia is an anonymous bulletin board that changes by the millisecond. That is because anyone can participate and "anyone" includes Neo-Nazis on Wikipedia who delete historic documentary film footage and other factual material showing Dr. Curry's work (regarding the U.S. as the origin of the notorious stiff-armed gesture via the military salute in the early Pledge of Allegiance; and the swastika as alphabetical symbolism for socialism). Wikipedia is notorious for displaying lies despite the efforts of many other noted historians and writers (including Timothy Messer-Kruse, John Seigenthaler, Philip Roth) to correct the glaring falsehoods.

From the Tampa Bay Times Newspaper (TBT): **"Hi Dr. Curry, Thanks for your help today on our column exposing the early salute of the Pledge Of Allegiance."** (with columnist Robyn Blumner).

Despite the thank you note, TBT covers up the National Socialist German Workers Party and the origin of its dogma, symbols, and rituals. Perhaps that is because the TBT building is adorned with swastikas and a huge U.S. flag put on a pole out front every day.

After the writer Daniel Ruth was fired by the Tampa Tribune (another bay area newspaper), TBT hired him. They did so despite his history of Nazi-style name-calling. After Ruth's loss in a public debate challenge the local response against the crackpot was so great that Ruth said he was labeled a "Dork, anti-free market statist, $#%!&, Dummkopf, liberal, daffy, dolt, stupid, dunce and, oh by the way, socialist."

The goal of both newspapers has always been to expand the existing socialist police state, and to do so by keeping their readers (both of them) ignorant. That is why the Dead Writers Club put the Tribune out of business. TBT is not doing well either.

Dr. Curry is cited in the book "By Faith Isaac" from the author Elsa Henderson (November 1, 2013).

16. FIGHT THE PAST & PRESENT

Two embarrassing "Pledge of Allegiance" cases from the U.S. Supreme Court are: Minersville School District v. Gobitis, 310 U.S. 586 (1940); and West Virginia Board of Education v. Barnette, 319 U.S. 624 (1943). Minersville/Gobitis originated in 1935 and held that children could be persecuted for refusing the robotic incantation and the one-armed salute of the Pledge of Allegiance. Minersville/Gobitis was not overturned until the case of Barnette (1943). It was one of the fastest self-reversals by the U.S. Supreme Court.

People similar to the Gobitis kids were being persecuted in Germany and the USA at the same time. The National Socialist German Workers' Party had been in existence since 1920, and had electoral breakthroughs in 1930, and dictatorship in 1933. At the time (1940) when the Gobitis decision upheld mandated daily chanting of the socialist's pledge in the USA, the German socialists were allies with Soviet socialists in a pact to divide up Europe, invading Poland together, spreading WWII, and leading to the socialist Wholecaust (of which the Holocaust was   a   part).

Government schools (socialist schools) have been a part of every police state in the past. Government schools remain a part of the police state and they have police officers permanently assigned within the schools today. Government schools are unconstitutional for that reason, and for many other reasons, including the following:

1.   Government schools violate the First Amendment right to freedom of speech and freedom of the press. The government schools (socialist schools) tell everyone what to think and say and write.   The pledge is part of that indoctrination. Schools will not teach children that they can refuse the pledge, but bully them into obedience every day.

2.   Government schools violate everyone's right to due process of law and to a fair jury trial. Government schools tell everyone to submit to taxation/theft and socialism, to submit to unjust laws, and to render verdicts of "guilty" against people charged with unjust laws.

3.   Government schools violate the 4th Amendment right against unreasonable searches and seizures. They will not teach students to exercise their right to remain silent, and to refuse answer questions from police and other government employees; to refuse to consent to searches of their persons,

possessions, lockers, and cars. Government schools evade the "expectation of privacy" standard that exists outside of schools. Schools are day-prisons for kids.

All students (and all adults) should learn to evade the police state. The way to evade the police state is: evade the police.

Do not talk to the police.

Do not consent to any search of any kind.

Do document encounters with police by video recording them. Police officers are often video recorded during traffic stops. The videos are often recorded on cell phones by drivers who are stopped by police. Other videos are recorded by dashboard cameras installed on police cars, or by body cameras worn by police officers.

Video recordings of police are often posted to the world wide web on the internet and viewed by millions of civilians. Some videos expose illegal searches, improper arrests, shocking violence, thefts, corruption, and more. The videos make drivers want to avoid becoming victims of the USA's police state.

Any driver who cannot afford to install a video recording system in his/her car should visit a thrift store and buy broken cameras that look like digital recording cameras. The cameras can be positioned using velcro in the rear window and on the dashboard above the steering wheel facing toward where police stand outside of the driver's window. The rear window camera serves as a warning sign to discourage some police from even pulling a car over. If a cop does approach the

163

driver's window, the driver can gesture at the cameras and state "I have cameras" (which technically is not a lie, even though the cameras don't function).

Drivers should pro-actively prevent cops from following behind them in traffic. Police have ticket and arrest quotas that have led to the planting of drugs, to corruption, and to deaths.

If you are able to see a cop in your rear view mirror (no matter how far back the cop is), then you should turn and either take a different route, or circle the block, or pull into a gas station or convenience store.

If you are on the highway and it is possible to take an exit, then do so. If possible, re-enter the highway after the officer has passed.

If there is a cop at an intersection ahead of you in a position where you will pass and he might end up behind you, preemptively turn before you pass the cop's location. Change your route, or circle the block so that the cop will have proceeded elsewhere, or so that he will be ahead of you.

It should go without saying: Don't ever pass a cop. If a cop appears in front of you, then you should remain a long way back, or take a different route. Don't pass.

If you turn and the officer follows you, then you should immediately find a place to stop (e.g. pull into a gas station, convenience store, or fast food location, then exit the car and go inside).

In other words prevent cops from being in a position to read your tag, and prevent them from being in a position to pull you over.

At night, it is difficult to identify police cars from a distance. Many people minimize night driving in order to avoid having a police car sneak up on them.

Similar prophylactic behavior is wise at home: if there is a knock at the door and the person knocking is a cop (or looks like a bureaucrat or anyone from the government), do not answer the door. Do not speak. Wait for the person to leave.

The information above might save your life and the lives of those who are with you.

17. UN-EARTHING POLICE DOG FRAUD

Drug dogs are used for lies. They are used to fabricate "probable cause" to search cars (and other conveyances, objects, and packages).

Judges write clueless opinions in which they wonder about how accurate drug dogs are, and they overlook this point: Police can lie and say that the dog alerted when the dog did not alert at all. It does not matter how accurate drug dogs are.

The most common excuse for police dogs is modern prohibition: the insane War on Drugs.

The word "police" is related to the word "policy" because police enforce the policies of deranged politicians on the local, state, and federal level.

The word 'politics' is derived from the word 'poly' meaning 'many', and the word 'ticks' meaning 'blood sucking parasites.'

Blood-sucking parasites on dogs compare favorably to

166

blood-sucking parasites who use dogs for lies in order to steal millions of dollars from law-abiding citizens under the police state and its Civil Forfeiture laws.

Cops lie like dogs. Cops lie like rugs. According to grammar rules, the second sentence is ungrammatical because, for rugs, the word should be "lay," and not "lie." And dogs are not dishonest, but they do want to lie on the floor. Cops tell lies about drug dogs, and they use drug dogs to tell lies about humans. Perhaps this tweaks it: Cops lie like a dog on a rug during a July day in Florida. In other words, they lie a bunch.

Drug dogs are natural libertarians with no interest in modern prohibition, and they have to be constantly taught and reinforced (brainwashed) to detect drug odors, and to approach peaceful humans and search them, so that humans can be arrested, handcuffed, and imprisoned for decades. That is not an easy trick to teach a dog. It is easier to teach humans.

Drug dogs are a reminder of similar police-state tactics and obsessive Gestapo behavior under the National Socialist German Workers Party.

Police officers should not be forced to endanger their own lives (and the lives of innocent dogs) enforcing modern prohibition and initiating violence against peaceful people engaged in non-violent consensual conduct.

The following paragraphs describe how narcotics dogs are used as ruses against humans, to violate constitutional rights against searches and seizures -

* NEVER CONSENT TO A SEARCH. Consenting to a search

means that the driver is waiving his rights under the Fourth Amendment of the U.S. Constitution. If consent is given, and the police either find or fabricate a reason for an arrest, then any motion to suppress based on an illegal search will be opposed by the prosecution with the truthful argument that the victim/defendant "consented" and waived his rights. If a victim/defendant consents and then tells his lawyer "they had no reason to search my car," part of the lawyer's response will include this: "It does not matter because you consented to the search. You waived your rights. That makes it more difficult for me to help you."

*Cops ask to search cars for no reason at all during routine traffic stops. Cops ask to search because they know that most victims are ignorant about the fact that drivers should "just say 'NO!'" (most drivers are know-nothings about constitutional rights). Drivers who do know are often too frightened or meek to say "NO!"

It is unknown how often cops ask for consent to search. It is unknown how often consent is given under duress or ignorance. Drivers who do not complain roadside will not complain later, and will not learn, and will not litigate later.

The police use of "consent searches" has inspired opponents of the practice to educate the public with the slogan "Say No To Searches!" and "Say No To The Police State."

* If drivers say "no," then cops tell drivers that a K-9 unit has been requested by police radio, and a sniffer dog is coming to

the scene, and that a longer ordeal is therefore inevitable if the driver will not "consent" to a search of the car. That warning is often a lie to induce consent. There is no police dog on the way.

* Whether or not a dog is in transit, some cops add additional lies to make drivers think that there will be a long wait, and that the driver must stay until a dog arrives. Cops rely on driver ignorance of the fact that evidence will be suppressed if drivers are detained longer than it takes to complete the traffic stop (e.g. write the ticket). Drivers are induced to consent to search to avoid a long wait based on lies. Cops will say things like "You should consent to search, because the dog is going to scratch your car up," which is a threat of property damage made to induce consent, and it is also an indication of a badly trained drug dog (if it is true), and a bad handler.

* Learn to say "AM I UNDER ARREST? OR AM I FREE TO GO?" Some cops let drivers think that they are obliged to stay even when the cop has no reason to detain drivers any longer. Cops rationalize that drivers inexplicably loiter roadside with cops, or that drivers enjoy waiting for dog sniffs. Cops take advantage of drivers who are too stupid (or too meek) to ask if they are free to go, so that drivers "consent" (in the rationalization of cops) to unwarranted detention by not leaving.

* Cops lie about how long it takes to write tickets or to obtain a

radio response on a tag inquiry, or license inquiry. If a dog is actually en route, then some cops write tickets very slowly, until the dog arrives.

* Even after the dog arrives at the scene of a traffic ticket stop, cops still try to obtain "consent to search" because cops think that they can more easily avoid suppression of evidence motions that expose the cop's falsehoods, reveal the dog's inaccuracy, destroy the dog's future credibility, and force the dog to be retired, and necessitate a new dog (puppet) to replace it (until that new dog is exposed). With the dog at the scene, cops will repeat statements such as "You should consent to search, because the dog is going to scratch up your car."

*What happens if a dog is discredited in a court proceeding that reveals the dog to have a high error rate? There appears to be little that prevents police from re-naming the dog, moving it to another location, or taking other actions to continue using the dog for its originally intended purpose: as a ruse to fabricate "probable cause" for searches.

*Another reason why police use drug dogs is the same reason why felons use large menacing dogs: as substitutes for guns, in order to threaten and terrorize people. Video recordings of some drug dogs makes it appear as if they have been trained to bark continuously and to leap and lunge. Some "drug dogs" are also trained to be attack dogs. That can be dangerous if the dog becomes confused about its purpose in a particular situation

170

involving a civilian.

* Police ask for consent because they have no "probable cause" to search. When victims persist in refusing to consent to a search, police take advantage of court cases from judges who opine that police can gain "probable cause" if a properly trained and properly handled drug dog gives a bonafide "alert" indicating that the dog smells the presence of illegal contraband in the car. A search is forced against the driver's will.

*Police fabricate "probable cause for a search" by lying and claiming that a canine alerted, when the dog did not alert. A search is then forced against the driver's will. Video recordings on the web show these police lies, including videos where the dog handler walks the dog to the front of the victim's car (where the dog handler deliberately hides from the police car's dashboard camera), and the dog handler loudly proclaims that the dog is alerting, while there is no view of any alert by the dog on the video.

If drugs are not found hidden at the front of the car (and drugs usually are not found there) then that fact should be used in a motion to suppress evidence because it shows that the dog did not alert, or that the dog's alert was an error. The same argument should be made whenever drugs are not found near the spot where a drug dog allegedly alerted on the car.

*Police manufacture "probable cause for a search" by cuing a drug dog, to induce it to "alert," if the dog is not alerting on its own. Police lie and claim that the dog properly alerted. A search is forced against the driver's will. Victims need to pay close attention to the dog and its handler, make a video recording (and also use any police dash camera recording) to expose the truth.

Cuing can be deliberate or subconscious (dogs may imagine that the handler desires the dog to alert). Sometimes it is not clear whether the cue is deliberate or subconscious. For example, if a dog handler repeatedly walks the dog around a car it could be cuing that is deliberate or subconscious. The handler might know from past experience that if he walks the dog around the car enough, the dog will eventually interpret that as a cue and alert. Motions to suppress evidence should argue that a dog should circle a car once (because if drugs dog are as amazingly accurate as cops claim, then one circle is enough). Any additional circling is cuing (because the cop is angry that the dog did not alert on the first walk).

* Many errors by drug dogs cause lawyers to wonder if police carry drugs to plant scents so that drug dogs will alert. Some news items support such speculation in cases where drugs have been planted by police. Drug prohibition is wrong, and its wrongfulness is compounded by government during enforcement of "modern prohibition."

* If a narco dog alerts and nothing is found in the resulting search, then cops will never record that as an error by the dog.

If confronted by the apparent error under cross-examination, cops will testify (testi-lie) that the dog detected lingering odors of contraband that were recently present. Cops will testify that dogs never make mistakes, never have and never will, and that apparent errors are, in reality, the dog's skillful detection of residual odors of contraband.

No one can question a dog about whether the cop is lying or mistaken, and it is usually a waste of time to ask a cop the same types of questions.

Police like dogs because the dogs cannot be cross-examined. Defendants are denied their constitutional right to confront witnesses against them.

A motion to suppress should be filed because experts will testify that drug dogs can be trained (and should be trained) to ignore residual odors. Dogs that are not trained to ignore residual odors should be considered incompetent to provide probable cause for a search.

* Motions to suppress in court should argue that the drug dogs cannot provide probable cause because "drugs are everywhere." Drugs are on the ground (in restaurants, bars, streets) and can transfer to shoes when people step on the wrong spot. Drugs are then transferred to cars from shoes. Drugs can be on the ground underneath the spot where a car is stopped by police. Drugs are on roads and in parking lots and can transfer to the tires and underbelly of passing cars (this is an explanation of why a dog would alert on parts of a car where no drugs are found). Drugs are in the air, blown by the

173

wind, to land on passing cars. Drugs can be in the rain that falls on cars and dries, leaving a residue. Drugs can be on the hands and clothing of police from earlier arrests. Drugs are on paper money and then transferred to the hands, pockets and clothing of innocent people who handle the money later.

* Drug dog fraud is about more than cops stealing drugs. It is also about cops stealing cars, money and other valuables. Under the police state's civil forfeiture laws, police will lie and claim that large sums of money are "drug money." Police will steal the money, even if no drugs were found and no arrest was made. Police will bolster their lies that the money is drug money with additional lies that a dog alerted on the car (even if no drugs were found). Police use civil forfeiture laws to steal cars, money, real estate, and other valuables. Under civil forfeiture laws, police can engage in theft without finding drugs, without filing any criminal charges, and without convicting anyone of a crime. Regardless of any criminal charges, the theft of the victim's property becomes a separate nightmare.

18. NARCOTICS DOG TRAINING

Drug dogs are similar to humans in that dogs must be taught to approach peaceful people and search them, so that humans can be arrested, handcuffed, robbed, kidnapped, and imprisoned for decades under modern prohibition. That is not an easy trick to teach a dog. It is easier to teach humans.

Sniffer dog skills are often overestimated because people anthropomorphize dogs.

A dog's skills should be under-estimated because the most human-like quality that dogs have is that they are natural libertarians with no interest in the war on drugs.

Drug dogs are trained by playing a game. The dogs are taught using toys. The toys are hidden with drugs to trick the dog into a game of searching for its toy by associating the toy with drug odors.

A drug dog's training is not unique or complicated. Many

canine house pets will search for a toy that is hidden under a sofa pillow or a coffee can. The toy can be hidden with a package of cinnamon or some other item with a unique odor. After a few weeks, the cinnamon can be hidden alone, without the toy, and the dog will find the cinnamon via its smell, a smell that the dog was taught to associate with its toy.

Many errors can happen due to the training method. There is always the danger that a drug dog will alert on anything that resembles or smells like its toy (towels, tennis balls, car carpet, etc.).

Errors occur if a dog smells anything it desires or wants to attack or investigate: if a cat was carried in the car; if another dog has ridden in the car; if there is the odor of food in the car.

A Reuters news report stated that a San Diego arena was evacuated for about two hours, delaying a first-round game in the hugely popular national college basketball championship, after a hot dog cart attracted the attention of a bomb-sniffing dog. Thousands of fans arriving for a game between Marquette University and the University of Alabama were kept outside. Authorities cordoned off part of the building. It was meat, and not explosive heat, attracting the dog's attention.

Many drug dogs are so inaccurate that they could be replaced with the "drug coin." Flip the "drug coin" and if it lands on "heads," then that means that there is an alert and that there is probable cause to search. If it lands on "tails," then that means there is no alert, and that there is no probable cause (but a search occurs anyway).

Drugs dogs often bark up the wrong tree. In the U.S.

Supreme Court case of *Illinois v. Cabelles*, Justices Souter and Ginsburg dissented, pointing to studies showing that drug dogs frequently return false positives (12.5 to 60% of the time, according to one study).

Sniffer dogs are trained to detect only specific contraband (e.g. cocaine and marijuana). Some dogs are trained to detect only a single drug (e.g. only marijuana). To attack a K-9, determine what drug(s) it was trained to detect. If an arrest was made based on an alert for a substance that the dog was not trained to detect, then that should be part of a motion to suppress arguing that the alert was an error, or that it was a lie. One example would be: if a dog trained to detect only marijuana allegedly alerts and a search reveals only cocaine, then an arrest will occur for the cocaine despite the apparent error by the dog. Police will not volunteer any information about the fact that the dog was only trained to detect marijuana.

If an arrest is made based on a search by a drug dog, then a motion to suppress the evidence should be filed based on the arguments in this book including any evidence of cuing, the behavior of the dog at the scene, inadequate training of the dog, inadequate maintenance of the dog's training, a history of false positives (or a lack of record keeping regarding the dog's false positive rate) and various other problems that might be evident based on the timing and conditions during the detention of the victim and the search.

If a search occurs via the use of a drug dog, and no arrest occurs, then the police should be sued civilly based on the arguments in this book.

Under the current statist quo [sic], if contraband is found then the arrest will probably stand. If nothing is found, the driver leaves shaken, but there are few cases where the driver complains or sues. Bad police are emboldened by the fact that people will not take action after bad searches.

It doesn't matter whether a drug dog is accurate. The dog is present at the scene as a cover-up so that when the officer is called to testify he will "testalie" in court. Dogs are perfect pets for perjury.

Any case that lacks a videotape of a dog's actions on the scene should result in rejection of testimony that the dog alerted, or that the dog alerted without cueing.

Drug dogs differ from humans in that the natural libertarianism of drug-dogs always resurfaces, and must be suppressed constantly by law enforcement retraining. Without constant reinforcement, the dogs lose interest any skills they actually have will deteriorate further.

Record-keeping is indispensable in order to know whether dogs are guessing, or seeing cues. A record must be kept of every instance when the dog alerts and whether drugs were found. That is the only way to know the dog's error rate (how often the dog provides false positives) or to discover whether the dog is merely used for official lies. Only with record keeping and independent testing can any judge draw any conclusion from the dog's "game playing" out on the street.

Any criminal case with inadequate record-keeping about a dog should result in suppression of the evidence and dismissal of the charges against the defendant.

Dogs approximate humans in that they go along with the system to avoid disapproval from peers. Humans crave approval from supervising officers, other police, teachers, classmates, friends, et cetera. Drug dogs crave approval from their police handlers. Dogs play the game, and will try to guess and read cues (subconscious cues or deliberate cues), because the dogs are searching for approval, not for drugs.

Dogs mimic humans in that they can be trained (brainwashed) to do hurtful things – such as passing the 18th amendment (the old prohibition) in the case of humans. In the dogged pursuit of modern prohibition, some dogs are slow learners, as are some humans.

The government's war on drugs is a dog chasing its own tail.

Let's liberate drug dogs. Return them to protecting people from violence and theft, which is also the only proper purpose of law enforcement. Dogs should be man's best friend, not man's persecutor.

19. HISTORY OF DRUG DOGS

Drug dog fraud was encouraged in January 2005, under the U.S. Supreme Court case of *Illinois vs. Caballes* (not one of Dr. Curry's cases), holding that a dog sniff during a traffic stop was not a "search." *Caballes* involved a allegedly "legitimate" traffic stop for speeding (that turned into 12 years in prison for marijuana).

Caballes is interpreted to mean that cops can take dogs fishing. *Caballes* and similar cases turn canines into props for lies. When dogs are used as props for lies, it doesn't matter whether dogs are well-trained.

The *Caballes* case from the U.S. Supreme Court foreshadows more police-state possibilities: Uniformed law enforcement marching through neighborhoods with German shepherds on leashes sniffing anything and everything -every car parked on or near the street, the air emanating from homes, neighbors walking outside.

Imagine the same thing at any place of business or employment, and police marching German shepherds through parking lots, car to car, for no reason other than fishing expeditions. Imagine the same nightmare in any shopping area or a downtown street area, a festival, a bar's parking lot. Uniformed agents with German shepherds sniffing pedestrians and their bags and cars and anything. The uniformed harassing the uninformed searching purses, pockets, cars, et cetera, on the streets.

Police-state tactics were witnessed worldwide via videotape from Stratford High School in Goose Creek, South Carolina, where police used dogs in a surprise "raid" for students inside of a school.

No drugs were found in the raid of the Goose Creek school.

In other schools, classes have been interrupted and the children were marched out and lined up to be harassed by a dog.

What next? Cops with barking German Shepherds marching through classrooms every morning to sniff each child during the robotic chanting of the Pledge of Allegiance in the police-state camps known as government schools. If so, that would give the government another excuse to re-impose the Pledge of Allegiance's earlier Nazi salute. That will be another way in which the U.S. police state resembles the National Socialist German Workers Party (Nazis).

The police state in the U.S. is nothing new. Francis Bellamy (author of the Pledge of Allegiance, and the origin of the Nazi salute and Nazi behavior) wrote the pledge to promote the government's takeover of schools. Bellamy was a self-proclaimed socialist and touted (along with his cousin Edward Bellamy) what he called "military socialism."

The Bellamy cousins wanted government to use socialized schools to achieve their goals. They inspired trite propaganda in which every "problem" spirals into a war: the War on Drugs, the War on Poverty, the War on Crime, the War on Illiteracy, the War on Terrorism, et cetera. They inspired the use of government force and violence for any and all purposes. Today, the U.S.'s military-socialist complex and its aggressive military socialism is the Bellamy dogma.

The government's schools will not teach children about their Constitutional rights, including their 4th Amendment rights against searches (including the right to refuse to consent to searches, to say "NO!" to searches), and their right to remain silent (to refuse to answer questions when a police officer barks at them).

The Pledge of Allegiance is obedience training for humans: stand, speak, sit, roll over, attack, play dead.....

Guardians of groupthink believe that any American who "loves freedom" must chant hypnotically, salute and sing whenever someone barks a command to do so.

20. POLICE DOG RESEARCH

In an article entitled "Free the Drug Dogs!" at the History News Network (of George Mason University) the writer Keith Halderman stated, *"... attorney Rex Curry, who was one of the first libertarians I ever met, and who helped transform much of my thinking, developed a case that may be headed to the Supreme Court. [The case], which he won, involves a challenge to the veracity of drug dogs searches. The state of Florida is appealing and the issue is on the high court's docket."*

A professional dog trainer wrote about Dr. Curry: *"... you did our profession a great favor. Maybe we can get rid of the B.S. trainers and the monkey-see-monkey-do method to training, and apply the science behind it."*

DrugSense Weekly journal published an interview asking, *"Given the problems with drug dogs explored in your work, why do you think they are so popular with police departments and municipal government?"*

Dr. Curry's answer was, *"Oh that is easy. You have to remember that there is a strong incentive for law enforcement not to CARE whether the dogs are accurate. The dogs can simply be props for lies, in that the dogs are there to overcome refusals to consent to search, and the dog provides law enforcement officers (LEOs) with the ability to say that an alert occurred even if there was no alert. And here is another angle: some LEOs do not want a 'drug dog,' they want a 'car dog,' in that they want a dog that when shown a car will alert, as if to say 'yes that is a car.' For some LEOs the goal is to search whenever the LEO desires, period. The dog is simply a ruse to do so. That is why the dogs are so popular. Do not be confused with the idea that there are 'problems with drug dogs.' For some LEOs those are not problems at all. And again, that is why some LEOs have no interest in maintaining records about their dogs."*

Many people write with responses to the ongoing research about drug dogs, including this one: *"I discovered a vacant lot where some dog-cops were meeting and I saw them signal training the dogs to 'GO OFF' on cue with very slight hand motions. Then I saw them walk dogs around a COP car they used (this shows it will work in any situation) and when the cop made this little twitch with one finger extended, the dog would bite at the door handle and tires and stand on its back legs and bark at the windows etc..."*

The Libertarian Lawyer was interviewed about drug dogs in Playboy magazine, and that prompted another drug dog expert to quip: *"Dr. Curry made it in to Playboy Magazine without taking his clothes off."*

The police state (and the use of drug dogs) is becoming an international problem, as evidenced by this excerpt of a communication from abroad:

"I wonder if I could please ask for some help? We are a children's civil rights organisation based in the UK. As you are probably aware, there has been a rise in the use of drugs sniffer dogs here. In some schools, dogs are taken in to perform routine searches, and it is now commonplace in London to have dogs posted at the exits to London underground trains.

While we have been concerned about the use of dogs, and had objected on various civil liberties grounds, we had naively assumed that dogs were pretty accurate! We've found out the hard way that this isn't true: two of our (non-drug-using) teenaged members have now been stopped by dogs at stations, and then searched. They were both pretty upset by the experience.

We want to find all the research possible about the accuracy of sniffer dogs, and intend to bring out a report to publicise what is going on. – quite honestly, we are more likely

*to stop the practice of going into schools with dogs in this way,
rather than by arguing civil liberties (not a major concern of
the British public!)* [from "Action on Rights for Children"]

The description of the police-state in the U.K. (from the
comments above) are similar to the U.S.'s police state. People
in Britain and worldwide witnessed police-state tactics in the
U.S. via videotape from Stratford High School in Goose Creek,
South Carolina, where police used dogs in a surprise "raid" for
students inside of a school. Those images are available in any
web search.

Similar behavior may be in store for the UK if it has not
already happened there.

A lawyer revealed: *"A judge in my local county was
stopped for speeding and was treated like dirt by the cop.
That's one judge who woke up."*

Government's attitude toward your liberty is like a dog at a
fire hydrant. The difference is that the government will pee on
your head and tell you that it is raining.

Don't "Howl Hitler" – instead, stop the U.S.'s police state.

21. LOCK YOUR DOORS

Big banks advise their employees to do the following after the bank is robbed and the robber has left:: rush to all doors and lock them immediately. The advice is intended to prevent the robber from returning and taking hostages, or taking lives.

There is more to the explanation that the banks don't tell employees: If there are police outside, they might shoot at the robber and drive him back inside the bank. Police can turn what would have been a short incident, into a protracted killing spree. If the robber runs back inside the bank, hours might elapse before police decide to "rush" in. During those hours, people who are already injured might bleed to death; other people might be executed or injured by the robber; the newly injured victims might bleed to death waiting for police help.

That is why banks advise employees to lock the door BEFORE calling police. Locking the door is the very first action to take. Do not alert police until AFTER the doors are locked. Locking the door is more important than notifying police, because police might make things worse.

The advice of the banks applies anywhere that a violent attack occurs: bars, restaurants, night clubs, dance venues, stores, or anywhere. After an attack occurs and the criminal has fled, the doors need to be locked until it is clear that the criminal is far away or dead. There are many examples of police causing a violent criminal to re-enter and take hostages and kill more victims; and causing people who were already injured to bleed to death waiting for aid.

Even if the criminal has left, or has committed suicide, the police might not know it, and they will sometimes wait a long time before entering a safe location. Police will order injured people to remain inside, where the injured will bleed to death waiting for police help.

Locking the door is especially important in any government-mandated "gun-free" zone, where the government has disarmed the victims. Governments often disarm their victims. Victims were disarmed by Stalin, Mao, Hitler, Pol Pot, North Korea et cetera.

Victims are disarmed in Florida at bars and nightclubs. Places that sell alcohol are often forced to be "gun-free zones" under state laws. 49 people were killed and 53 were wounded in a government-mandated gun-free zone in Orlando, Florida in 2016. Much of the killing occurred after the criminal re-entered the area of his initial attack, after he fled from police near the front exit route, according to some accounts (as of the time this was written, government officials will not divulge the details). The culprit was driven deeper into the building where he took hostages and murdered more people over the course of hours before police attacked. Some victims died while waiting for medical help during the tragedy.

An astonishing part of the Florida disaster is that none of the customers in the bar had a gun. There is a high price to pay for obeying laws that restrict self defense. Socialists force many people to remit that steep payment, as under Stalin, Mao, and Hitler.

Some bars are so rough that a bouncer at the front entrance frisks everyone for weapons and will not allow entry to anyone who has a weapon.

Other bars are even rougher. At the roughest bars, if the bouncer frisks you and discovers that you are NOT carrying a gun, then he loans you one. If you don't have a gun, then you are not allowed to enter.

Some state legislatures are considering statutes that would require a person to carry a gun into places where laws now ban guns (e.g. dance clubs). They think that civilians need to be nudged to defend themselves. Only stupid people go into dangerous places without a gun. Some people learn the hard way and pay with their lives.

The police would not go into such places without a gun. Why should you? Cops are exempt from laws that disarm everyone else.

After a shooting incident there are often public comments from the worst active homicidal maniac in the USA (the President). His/Her body piles (including children, women, and other innocent non-combatants) while in office exceed that of any shooter in the nation ever. Add to that the death and misery during his/her earlier political career expanding military socialism and the police state. He/She makes arrestable serial killers seem angelic in comparison. Comedy ensues when the Commander in Chief pontificates in press conferences about "why are people so violent?" That butcher is surrounded 24/7 by men with guns (and more), and wants to reduce your ability to defend yourself against anyone (including him/her).

The above is why you should do what the police do: arm yourself. It is a reminder of the book entitled: "Dial 911 and Die." When seconds count, the police are only minutes away. And even if the police are closer than minutes away, they might cause more casualties.

22. PAST & FUTURE POLICE STATE

Officer Allen pulled his patrol car onto Central Avenue. As usual, all the traffic ahead of him began turning off of Central Avenue. Within moments, the avenue was empty. Allen drove for a about a mile and then turned north (right) onto Main Street. Again, all the cars ahead of him began turning off of Main Street until he was alone.

Officer Allen looked in his rear-view mirror and in the distance he could see some cars cautiously re-entering the street in back of him and keeping a large distance, pacing him from behind, never approaching, never passing.

He remembered when it didn't used to be this way. People were different until that day when a meme was posted on the internet. This is that meme:

191

Never let a police car advance into a position where the police officer can signal for you to stop. Drivers should pro-actively prevent cops from following them in traffic.

If you are able to see a cop in your rear view mirror (no matter how far back the cop is), then you should turn and either take a different route, or circle the block, or pull into a gas station or convenience store.

If you are on the highway and it is possible to take an exit, then do so. If possible, re-enter the highway after the officer has passed.

If there is a cop at an intersection ahead of you in a position where you will pass and he might end up behind you, preemptively turn before you pass the cop's location. Change your route, or circle the block so that the cop will have proceeded elsewhere, or so that he will be ahead of you.

It should go without saying: Don't ever pass a cop. If a cop appears in front of you, then you should remain a long way back, or take a different route. Don't pass.

If you turn and the officer follows you, then

you should immediately find a place to stop (e.g. pull into a gas station, convenience store, or fast food location, then exit the car and go inside).

In other words prevent cops from being in a position to read your tag, and prevent them from being in a position to pull you over.

The information above might save your life and the lives of those who are with you.

The meme above went viral and seemed to spread for years. Soon, it was altering the way people behaved, changing the way they drove.

But it worsened.

First it worsened at the strip clubs. The police had harassed the striptease clubs for decades. One day, a nude dance club put a lock on its entrance and dark tinting on the window next to the door. A doorman inside would hit a button to unlock the door for customers.

But they wouldn't let cops in.

And police outside could not see inside the club, or see if the doorman was there or who he was, or whether anyone was inside or not.

It was the buzz-in system that jewelry stores had used for years. Soon, the jewelry stores wouldn't let cops in either. At least not unless the jewelry store had just been robbed and specifically called for the police. Then they would let the cops in. But jewelry store robberies were rare.

Eventually, bars and other businesses began putting electronic buzzer locks on their doors and stopped letting in anyone who wore a uniform or looked like a bureaucrat.

It was time for lunch. Officer Allen pulled into an alley. He began to change his clothes to civilian attire.

It was the only way he could gain entry to a restaurant for lunch!.

23. GUNS & HISTORY

Police states disarm individuals in order to prevent resistance to socialism's violence and theft. Government schools (socialist schools) will not teach students about the 2nd Amendment, nor about firearms.

A recent school shooting was described as the worst massacre in American history. It added to the growing number of deaths attributable to government schools and those people who maintain existing gun laws that disarm the innocent. Even so, the number of deaths caused by the government in that school shooting was greatly exceeded by the government's death toll at Waco, Texas, a much worse massacre in American history.

School violence demonstrates that government's schools are unconstitutional under the Second Amendment right to self-defense against violent predators (whether such predators are in the government or out). Government's schools are victim disarmament zones and create ignorance of the Second Amendment Right to Keep and Bear Arms.

Martin Niemöller was famous for his poem "First they came..." and for his opposition to German socialism and its police state under Adolf Hitler. Niemöller's legacy also serves to remind everyone to oppose victim disarmament zones.

Niemöller, a German Protestant minister, was persecuted in Germany while it was under the influence of the National Socialist Workers Party of Germany (Nazi Party) and its socialist swastika. The charges were trumped up and he spent the duration of World War II in Dachau (where there were many other people - including other ministers, monks, nuns, and priests - many of whom did not survive). They had all been disarmed.

The beginning of Niemoller's verse is often mis-stated as "First they came for the Socialists." Niemoller never said "First they came for the Socialists..." (see the work of the historian Dr. Rex Curry). The ignorant use of the term "socialist" in the verse is common because of widespread ignorance that "Nazis" did not call themselves "Nazis" (they called themselves socialists). Niemoller was an early supporter of Hitler's socialism, so Niemoller would not have written "First they came for the socialists" (unless his poem was a cynical inside joke about how socialists have set world records killing other socialists as under Stalin and Soviet Socialism; Mao and Chinese socialism; Hitler and German socialism, et cetera. In that sense, the phrase would have been accurate).

196

Socialists lie about the poem (they use the "socialist" version) in order to cover-up the fact that Hitler's supporters called themselves "socialists" and did so while speaking and writing at length about their deadly dogma.

Some websites (e.g. Wikipedia) concede the "socialist" phrase's lack of support (on the wakipedia page entitled "First they came for..."), yet those websites fail to explain the illogic of the phrase. It is a glaring omission due to the cowardice of wannabe intellectuals. That failure exists because dedicated liars on wakipedia do not want to explain that Hitler's supporters called themselves "socialists."

Wakipedia begins by finessing the phrase as "First they came for..." in the title and leaving off the term "socialist." Yet, on Wakipedia's page for "Martin Niemoller" the false version ("First they came for the socialists...") tops the page, and the rest of the page is designed to hide the fact that "Nazis" did not call themselves "Nazis," but called themselves "socialists" (this is a common method of deceit throughout Wakipedia). Of course, Wakipedia changes by the millisecond, so by the time anyone reads this and views Wakipedia, its deceits might have been covered-up. Wakipedia tricks readers because its name rhymes with "Encyclopedia" (and its slogan is: "The Free Encyclopedia") even though it is merely an anonymous bulletin board where anybody can post anything (including lies and the lying liars who tell them). Wakipedia and other websites cover-up for socialism.

According to one interviewer, Niemoller (1892–1984) himself conceded that he did not use the term "socialist." No one can cite an original source for Niemoller using the term "socialist" in the popular misrepresentation of the poem.

Niemöller survived Germany's socialism, and it is odd to note that later in his life Niemöller seemed seduced by socialism despite his personal suffering under the socialist Wholecaust (of which the Holocaust was a part): ~50 million slaughtered under Soviet socialism; ~40 million slaughtered under Chinese socialism; and ~20 million slaughtered under German socialism.

Socialism demonstrates the importance of the individual right to own guns for self defense (against socialism, etc).

The same dogma permeated government schools (socialist schools) in the USA at that time. Indeed, the U.S. government followed Germany in becoming allies with Stalin and Soviet socialism. Socialist dogma continues to permeate the same schools today, and the Pledge of Allegiance is one example of it.

The Pledge of Allegiance was written by a socialist and it was the origin of the Nazi salute and Nazi behavior.

A better stiff-arm salute is one in which a gun is held in self-defense against violent attackers whether they are in the government or out. Guns rights stop violent socialism and violent socialists.

The following poem ("First They Came For The Machine Guns") was inspired by Niemöller's poem:

First they came for the machine guns, and I didn't speak up-because I had no machine guns.

Then they came for the "assault weapons," and I didn't speak up-because I had no assault weapons.

Then they came for the rifles, and I didn't speak up- because I had no rifles.

Then they came for the handguns, and I didn't speak up-because I had no handguns.

Finally, they came for my double-barreled shotgun- and I only managed to kill two of them.

(before they mowed me down with their machine guns, assault weapons, rifles, and handguns (while I was trying to reload)).

--- Libertarian History ---

24. NOT SEE NAZI SOCIALISM

Poetry about the (former) National Socialist German Workers Party:

To say "Nazi".....
to say & not see.
Not see Nazi reality.
not see, not see, Not See
Don't say "Nazi" !
Do not say and Not See
say "National Socialist German Workers' Party."

The preceding poem is about "Not-Sees." Modern "Not-Sees" are the ones who don't want people to see that Hitler and his supporters called themselves "Socialists" and that they did not call themselves "Fascists," nor "Nazis." That is why they will never point out that the swastika, although an ancient symbol, was used by German socialists to represent crossed

"S" letters for their dogma of socialism.

Hitler's symbol was a type of cross, a "Hakenkreuz" (hooked cross); he did not call it a "swastika." The misnomer "swastika" was used (and continues to be used) to cover up Nazism's origin in American Christian Socialism, via Francis Bellamy and his cousin Edward Bellamy (author of "Looking Backward" -the origin of the National Socialist movement).

There are many Not-Sees regarding the links of American socialism to German socialism, Italian socialism, Soviet socialism, Chinese socialism, and global socialism (e.g. links via the Bellamy cousins). There are also Not-Sees about the U.S.'s Pledge of Allegiance as the origin of the Nazi salute and Nazi behavior (see that and other discoveries revealed in the book "Pledge of Allegiance & Swastika Secrets").

Help expose Not-Sees. The preceding poem inspired the "Not Say Nazi" movement to stamp out widespread ignorance and to abolish the N-word and the F-word.

Not-Sees also want people to not see that Soviets called themselves "socialists." Not-Sees use the phrase "Stalin's Russia" in order to cover up the actual name of the country: Union of Soviet SOCIALIST Republics. If pressed, Not-Sees insist that the USSR was "communist," and Germany was "fascist," and they were complete opposites. Not-Sees never mention that German socialists and Soviets socialists were allies in a plan to divide up Europe, and invaded Poland together in 1939, launching the Socialist War (World War II), and leading to the socialist Wholecaust (of which the Holocaust was a part). If they mention that time at all, they only mention that the "Nazis invaded Poland," and they hope that the reader is ignorant about the alliance of German socialists and Soviet socialists.

25. TRAINING DOGS & LIZARDS

Earlier chapters in this book explained that a drug dog's training is not unique or complicated. Many canine house pets will search for a toy that is hidden under a sofa pillow or a coffee can. The toy can be hidden with an edible treat or some other item with a unique smell. After a few weeks, the snack can be hidden alone, without the toy, and the dog will find the snack via its odor, an odor that the dog was taught to associate with its toy, in a similar manner to how drug dogs are taught to associate the smell of a drug with their toys.

Yard lizards can be trained. The lizards look and behave like tiny Dachshunds. They can be trained to eat out of your hand. With enough training, they will climb up a lawn chair, jump in your lap and stare at you until you give them their favorite treat: mealworms.

Mealworms are available at most pet shops that sell snakes,

iguanas and other reptiles. The worms are sold in small plastic containers and they can be kept in the refrigerator for a month, where the worms stay dormant.

Mealworms make great conversation starters on salads.

Be sure to buy the smallest mealworms, about half an inch maximum length. Yard lizards, formally known as anoles (a-NO-lees), can't eat big mealworms.

Lizards also will eat live crickets; however, crickets jump about and are difficult to use in training.

To begin training, sit on the ground in an area where the lizards sun themselves and watch humans. If the mealworms have been refrigerated, let them warm up to reach maximum wiggliness. Wiggliness excites lizards.

Start by tossing the worms near the lizards and sit still while the lizard watches the worm wiggle and then rushes over to grab it. Then try placing the worms nearer to you, slowly closing the distance. Eventually, hold a wiggling worm in your fingers and lay your hand on the ground. Next, move on up to placing a wiggling worm on your forearm while laying your hand on the ground to serve as a staircase, so that the lizard can crawl up the arm to take the worm.

Some lizards are easier to train (hungrier) than others. I have been in yards where the lizards could be coaxed to take a worm from the hand in one sitting. In other yards, the lizards were skittish and required multiple sessions. Lizards are skittish in areas with cats that prey on them.

The very act of tossing a worm will scare away some lizards. In such yards, a worm can be slowly placed about one yard from a lizard, and within clear eye-shot of the lizard. The human should back off to let the lizard approach.

Soon, lizards will be happy to see you come outside, and will approach you and other humans. You can call to them and they will come trotting over to you.

They will chase each other and fight each other to win your worms. They will perform peculiar territorial dances wherein two lizards will circle each other repeatedly with their tails rhythmically curling. They will do other crude things for your viewing pleasure. A carefully placed mirror can also prompt lizards to engage in displays to their own reflections.

So, if your child says he wants a new pet, just buy him a box of mealworms open the back door and say "knock yourself out, kiddo!

26. DOG ECONOMICS 101

Peter was walking with his Doberman "Lobo." They had grown to love these woods over their six-years together.

Suddenly a deadly poisonous snake bit Lobo. Peter frantically pulled out his cell phone and was relieved to hear his dog's veterinarian answer. The vet calmed Peter and explained that although the bite is lethal without treatment, there is 100% cure by injection for $2000 if Peter rushes Lobo to the office.

A shocked expression came over Peter's face as he ended the call. The dog was prostrate on the ground whimpering, as if asking, "What will happen to me?"

Looking down at his dog, Peter explained, "The vet said you're gonna die."

27. HISTORY OF SOCIALIST PROGRAMS

Have socialists in your city created a "community bicycle program" (CBP)? Some cities turn abandoned bicycles into "community bicycles" available to anyone for temporary use in downtown areas.

Community bicycles are all painted one loud color to help users distinguish them from private bikes. Safety-orange is the color sprayed on by bureaucrats in some towns. Then they call it the "Orange Bicycle Program" (OBP).

In my town, it was a short-lived program. The orange bicycles went unused until they were stolen and, it is hoped, repainted.

Politicians are inspired by programs like "community bicycles," even though they never ride the bikes, nor use government buses, nor government schools.

The same officials will be inspired by these programs:

Community Umbrella Program: Everyone gets caught in the rain without an umbrella. This program attempts to solve that problem. It is unfortunate that "Honor system" umbrellas have been tried with results similar to that of "community bikes," in that the umbrellas are given permanent homes elsewhere. The theft problem might be reduced a tad by painting the umbrellas safety orange.

Community car and RV program: Rain, heat and other bad weather discourage use of community bikes. Confiscated and abandoned cars and recreational vehicles (RVs) can be painted Day-Glo orange and left with on/off starter switches (to prevent lost or stolen keys). The RV's would also allow folks to catch a nap or even stay overnight if necessary. Instead of a new government rail mass-transit boondoggle, it would be cheaper to leave enough orange cars about for all predicted rail-riders.

Community food, clothing and shelter programs: Food, clothing and shelter are the three basic necessities and the following programs address them:

Community Refrigerators: community bicycles make riders hot, thirsty and hungry. Old refrigerators can be painted orange, filled with food and beverages, and placed near street corners and bike stands so that riders, pedestrians and anyone else can avail themselves of food and drink, which could be eaten en route to another destination, leaving uneaten portions in another orange refrigerator for others, or for later. This program has the added advantage of allowing people to add their own food and drink to the refrigerators, thus contributing to the program and ensuring its success and longevity.

Community clothing program: Orange jumpsuits can be borrowed from nearby county jails where the orange clothing program is already being enjoyed by many residents (similar to the fashion of Guantanamo Bay detention camp), some of whom have already enjoyed the orange bike program. When the clothing is not being worn, it can be left in orange boxes attached to the top of the orange refrigerators, available to any other clothing-challenged persons.

Community Houses program: For the temporarily displaced. Instead of tearing down crack houses and condemned structures, paint them Day-Glo orange and add them to the other community programs. These free and open houses would work on the honor system, only to be used overnight or so long as it takes the user(s) to find "normal" housing.

28. WATER'S SOCIALIST PAST

This motion was actually filed in court against a citation (imposing a monetary fine) alleging lawn-watering on an improper date and time. The citation was dismissed.

MOTION TO DISMISS
WATER CONSERVATION CITATION
FOR IMPROPER LAWN WATERING

The undersigned Defendant moves to dismiss the "Water Conservation Citation" in this case which was recently issued for the alleged watering of a lawn on a day or time not specified by government edict.

This motion to dismiss would be filed with the same

arguments if, in addition to socializing water, the local government also socialized food, clothing, shelter, oil, phosphate, phone calls, electricity, lumber, land, milk, natural gas, gypsum, gasoline, football, coal, concrete, chalk, cement, computers, crops, cable TV, toilet paper, or any other goods and services. Those goods and services (food, clothing, shelter, et cetera) will hereafter be abbreviated -
"FCSOPHPHELLMNGGGFCCCCCCCTVTP"

   In support of this motion to dismiss, the Defendant states the following:

   FCSOPHPHELLMNGGGFCCCCCCCTVTP are a few examples of goods and services, besides water, that government is not supposed to own, sell, or monopolize. If Government sold the other items, it would cause the same disastrous results that it has caused in water: shortages, misery, soviet-style rationing and the use of police and courts to restrict everyone's purchases and uses. The more goods and services that government socializes, the more totalitarian society becomes.

   Government water is a true monopoly because the government bans competitors by law. In comparison, Bill Gates' computer company is not a monopoly here because there is no law that bans others from selling computers in the same geographical area. It is fortunate that the local government did not take over the computer business, or the same sad results would have occurred as they have with water: shortages, misery, soviet-style rationing of computers, a controlled internet, and the use of police and courts to restrict everyone's purchases and uses.

The government water monopoly creates the overuse problem and then tries to solve it with more antidisestablishmentarianism via "tiered pricing." Tiered pricing is price gouging under a socialistic system.

Water is too important for the government to be involved. Only under a free market system do higher prices encourage competitors to find and provide more water or other alternatives.

People who support watering rules are chumps who promote waste by propping up the socialized system, helping wasteful individuals evade the true costs of wastefulness, costs which would otherwise be levied in market prices among private firms just like other goods.

The government water monopoly is a violation of every individual's right to "life, liberty and the pursuit of happiness," and a violation of personal freedom and economic freedom.

The purpose of government is to recognize and protect private property rights in all resources, and to protect property rights from violence and theft, so that individuals are free to own and distribute water, food, clothing, shelter, oil, phosphate, phone calls, electricity, lumber, land, milk, natural gas, gypsum, gasoline, football, coal, concrete, chalk, cement, computers, crops, cable TV, toilet paper, and all other goods and services.

It is not the purpose of government to provide water, food, clothing, shelter or other goods and services, and any attempt by the government to do so always involves theft and violence. Government water involves police state tactics of soviet-style rationing in its most petty form. Government water involves theft and violence and is, therefore, illegal.

29. WOODMAN SPARE THAT OLD $10 TREE

Popular songs often misrepresent property rights and economic freedom. Such misrepresentations are sometimes intentional and other times result from sheer ignorance of free market economics. The famous song "Woodman, Spare That Tree" is an example.

The song tells the tale of how a sentimental man prevented the chopping of a familiar tree. The lyrics imply that the tree was saved by emotional pleas and even by an implied threat of violence against the woodman. The libertarian historian Dr. Rex Curry has pointed out that the poetic plea is pure fiction and omits the most important truth: the tree was saved because the woodman was paid $10 to not cut down his own tree on privately owned property.

The song originated from a poem written in 1837 by George Pope Morris, a well-known journalist and poet who founded the New York Mirror in 1823 with Samuel Woodworth. In 1830 Morris wrote that he and a friend were walking in Manhattan when they saw a tenant of a property preparing to cut down a "grand old elm" (the elm became an oak in the song) for firewood. As the story goes, Morris and his companion talked to the woodman and negotiated to pay him $10 to let the tree stand.

Morris' poem misrepresented the event in other ways, in addition to omitting the pecuniary act that actually saved the tree. If any of the parties present remembered the tree from childhood, it was more likely the anonymous woodman. And if any of the parties promoted the progress that removed trees from the landscape of Manhattan, it was Morris, founder of the New York Mirror, as much as the poor tenant.

Morris claimed that the elm tree was still standing as late as 1862.

However, economic myopia might have blinded Morris from seeing if the tenant used the $10 to start a new business, the Manhattan Firewood and Tree Clearing Corporation, which went on to make Manhattan a treeless wonderland, thanks to Morris' seed money. Morris was oblivious to the economic reality that the tenant presumably requested $10 in order to purchase an equal or greater amount of firewood from someone who presumably felled some other tree(s) somewhere else (say on the next block?). In other words, Morris' act may have resulted in the death of one or more older, grander trees elsewhere.

Morris' histrionic misrepresentation has misled many environmentalists who act as if every tree is priceless, as implied in Morris' poem. Yet Morris easily arrived at a price with the tenant and the price was only $10. A better title for Morris' poem would be "Money talks and whining walks."

Edward Bellamy repeated Morris' fiction in the article "Woodman, Spare That Tree!" for the newspaper where Bellamy was assistant editor (Springfield Daily Union, July 7, 1873: 4, col. 6). Bellamy was the notorious founder (1888) of "National Socialism" and "Military Socialism" in the United States. He was the cousin and comrade of Francis Bellamy, author of the Pledge of Allegiance (the origin of the Nazi salute and Nazi behavior, as revealed in the book "Pledge of Allegiance + Swastika Secrets").

The poem was set to music by Henry Russell and other musicians. Various examples of the melody can be found by searching the web.

To his credit, Irving Berlin, in comic fashion, restored a more accurate version of the story in the song "Woodman, Woodman, Spare That Tree!" from the Broadway Show "Ziegfield Follies of 1911" (Irving Berlin / Vincent Bryan).

Below are the lyrics to the Russell song. There are two alternate added stanzas authored by Dr. Curry. The first alternate stanza more completely describes the grand finale of free-market environmentalism that saved the tree. The second alternate stanza describes the sad situation of what most people do today with tree ordinances and watering restrictions. At the end is Irving Berlin's treatment of the original story.

Woodman, spare that tree!
Touch not a single bough!
In youth it sheltered me,
And I'll protect it now.
'Twas my forefather's hand
That placed it near his cot:
There, woodman, let it stand,
Thy axe shall harm it not!

That old familiar tree,
Whose glory and renown

Are spread o'er land and sea,
And wouldst thou hew it down?
Woodman, forbear thy stroke!
Cut not its earth-bound ties;
Oh, spare that aged oak,
Now towering to the skies!

When but an idle boy
I sought its grateful shade;
In all their gushing joy
Here too my sisters played.
My mother kissed me here;
My father pressed my hand --
Forgive this foolish tear,
But let that old oak stand!

My heart-strings round thee cling,
Close as thy bark, old friend!
Here shall the wild-bird sing,
And still thy branches bend.
Old tree! the storm still brave!
And, woodman, leave the spot:
While I've a hand to save,
Thy axe shall harm it not.

Here is the addendum that describes what actually

happened:

For woodman, see my hand,
ten dollars we agreed;
contracts are always grand
with private property.
both bill and tree are green,
and both are made of wood.
socialism is mean.
capitalism: good!

Here is the more likely modern addendum based on what people (especially those people inspired by Morris' misleading poem) actually do to each other today through tree ordinances, watering restrictions and other government action:

I rush to city hall
and socialists I'll find,
to steal your property
and treat it as mine.
We'll tell you what to do
with trees, water and all;
resistance will bring you
a costly vicious brawl!

--- Libertarian History ---

The following are Irving Berlin's Lyrics -

[1st verse:]
A great big tree grows near our house
It's been there quite some time
This tree's a slipp'ry elm tree and very hard to climb
But when my wife starts after me, up in that tree I roost
I go up like a healthy squirrel and never need no boost
The other day a woodman came to chop the refuge down
And carve it into kindling wood, to peddle 'round the town
I says to him, "I pray thee cease, desist, refrain and stop
Lay down that razor, man, chop not a single chop"

[Refrain:]
Woodman, woodman, spare that tree
Touch not a single bough
For years it has protected me
And I'll protect it now
Chop down an oak, a birch or pine
But not this slipp'ry elm of mine
It's the only tree that my wife can't climb
So spare that tree

[2nd verse:]
I said to him, "You see that hole
Up near that old treetop
I've got five dollars there, that's yours, if you refrain to chop

--- Libertarian History ---

No beast but me can climb that tree, 'cause it's too slippery
I can't get up myself, unless my wife is after me
So get my wife and I'll call her a very naughty word
And then you'll see me give an imitation of a bird
You may not know just where to go, when my wife gets around
But when she comes, remember this, if I'm not on the ground."

30. TREE LAWS MAKE TREES HISTORY

Lawyers are often consulted by property owners who want to remove trees without fear of tree-preservation laws. Attorneys cannot advise clients to ignore laws (though tree laws often seem easy to ignore). Clients can be told about what a lot of people do: they don't plant any trees that are protected by tree laws. And any tree protected in tree laws that is still small enough to be legally killed, is killed.

Tree laws make treeless property the safest route. That is because tree laws can be expanded in the future. Therefore, every existing tree is a potential risk that a property owner will be restricted by government in the future alteration of his property. Removing trees is the only way to be safe when tree laws are a possibility.

Tree laws kill trees, as every libertarian knows. And rightfully so, because tree laws violate private property rights by "socializing" trees.

The following is a popular joke about the endangered species act: if a property owner sees an endangered species on his property he should "shoot, shovel and shut up." The joke is based on the truth that if the government becomes aware of an endangered species on your private property, then you will lose your property rights, and be treated very badly.

Under tree-preservation laws the joke can be altered to warn property owners to "chop, chip and chill."

Tree laws illustrate the fatal conceit of socialism and its unintended consequences. Tree-huggers must have fallen out of a stupid tree and hit every branch on the way down. If public officials were any more stupid, they'd have to be watered weekly. If their antidisestablishmentarianism continues then more "protected" trees will die.

Tree laws prove that socialism is environmentally disastrous. Government built roads through forests, straightened rivers, drained wetlands, cut canals, and subsidized other agricultural uses with taxes and other socialism. The government has already done more environmental damage than private enterprise could ever have afforded to do.

Capitalism saves trees from socialism's destruction. Capitalists farm trees for paper, and other uses. Capitalists created alternative forms of power to replace the burning of wood.

The best environment is a capitalist environment. Mother Nature is a capitalist.

Trees prove that the color of a healthy environment and the color of money are the same. Capitalists are the true greens.

Even so, Government threatens tree owners on private property with tree laws. Tree laws fail to distinguish non-violent private acts from theft and violence. With tree laws, the government threatens theft and violence against peaceful people.

The following is poetry about a tree (or poetree) -

I think that I shall never see
a tree-law as beautiful as a tree
and if the tree-laws do not fall
I may not see a tree at all

31. HISTORY OF GOVERNMENT SCHOOLS

Once upon a time, there was a brave little boy named "Skippy" who decided to end bullying at his school. All the teachers at Francis Bellamy Elementary School were supportive when Skippy set a date to launch his anti-bullying campaign. He was going to give all the other children fun rubber wristbands colored red, white, and blue, with the embossed phrase "Say No to Bullies!" Small American flags on little sticks were similarly embossed. The fun freebies were patterned after the red, white, and blue colors of the giant flag painted on their school's exterior, the regular flags in each classroom, and after the large flag waving on the pole in front of their school.

When the big day came, Skippy was at school early in his homeroom class as the teacher began the day with the Pledge of Allegiance. The teacher, Miss Fulford, noticed that Skippy did not stand for the pledge as he always had in the past.

Miss Fulford interrupted the pledge and asked "Skippy, why do you remain seated during the Pledge of Allegiance?"

In his childish voice, Skippy said, "The Pwedge of Aweegiance is part of my campaign against bulwying. Children think that they have to chant the pwedge. The pwedge is the first bulwying that begins everwy day for wus."

"Do you have some new wacko religious beliefs that have turned you so naughty?" the teacher demanded of Skippy.

"No, Miss Fulford," said Skippy, "I wesearched the histowy. Nazi salutes came from the pwedge!"

"Well, we'll have none of that mister!" the teacher warned, "Even if you won't join everyone else, then you will stand up in respect, and keep your mouth shut!"

There was an awkward pause, as Skippy stared at the teacher, and the teacher glared at Skippy. Miss Fulford realized that Skippy would not move from his seated position. She pointed at the door and screamed, "TO THE PRINCIPAL'S OFFICE!"

Later that day, all the children rejoiced as they helped the school lynch Skippy. His lifeless body was left to hang from the flag pole, underneath the glorious star-spangled banner that Skippy would dishonor never more. As the sun set on Old Glory, the entire school (or rather, what remained of it) chanted the Pledge of Allegiance, as a murder of crows gormandized until they were satiated. Skippy's little feet and hands had been bound with his own kid-sized rubber bracelets that said "Say No To Bullies!"

--- **Libertarian History** ---

32. TRIANGLE SHIRTWAIST FACTORY FIRE

Ignacia Del Fuego typed during the morning break, finishing her manuscript about the Triangle Shirtwaist Factory fire that killed her grandmother and 145 other garment workers on March 25, 1911.

Gazing northeast from her 91st floor office in Manhattan, "Iggy" could see the area where the inferno occurred near Washington Square in Greenwich Village. Only the top three floors of the ten story building had been damaged in the fire; the refurbished "Brown Building" was now part of New York University. Two blocks from NYU is the apartment where Iggy resides with her eleven-year-old daughter, Brooke.

The final chapter of Iggy's book explained how the historic Shirtwaist fire, and her grandmother Frieda's untimely death, spurred legislation that improved safety for all.

"My book needs a grand finale," Iggy whispered to herself as her brown eyes fixed upon an odd plane on the horizon. It was flying fast and low. It was racing toward the towering office building next to hers.

Iggy screamed as the plane slammed into floors 94 through 98 of the northern facade next door. She had backed up to the far wall of her office as the fireball exploded hundreds of feet away from her.

Within moments, Iggy realized that, as in 1911, there was no municipal fire truck with rescue ladders that could reach those people above the conflagration in the adjacent building. The distance was ten times higher than her grandmother's garment factory. It was the first time that the thought had ever crossed Iggy's mind during the nine years she had occupied the skyscraper and written her manuscript.

During the fifteen minutes that Iggy stared in horror at the first tower, a second commuter jet slammed into her office tower from floors 78 through 84, only ten floors below Iggy's. The earthquake sent her staggering toward the stairs.

"Go up! Run to the roof!" yelled a feminine voice in the smoke-filled stairwell. Everyone was headed upward, and Iggy joined the rush.

At the top, the roof door was locked. It was another page from Grandma Frieda's requiem.

If the door had been unlocked, it would not have mattered because the government had no plan for helicopter rescues to the tallest buildings in Manhattan.

Everyone had assumed that the government was providing protection. That is why no one in the building had a BASE jump parachute (even though daredevils had parachuted from the towers many times in the past).

Smoke filled Iggy's lungs and she fought to remain upright. Iggy saw the outline of a young lady in the enveloping fumes. Iggy heard the girl sob, "Our government killed us. Its violence did this."

Iggy gasped, "Grandmother?" as she struggled to remain conscious, and watched the female walk toward a window that had shattered open.

At least 200 people fell or jumped to their deaths from the burning towers, landing on the streets and rooftops of adjacent buildings. Iggy was one of them.

Hours later, both buildings ceased to exist. The next day, Iggy was part of the soot and dust that coated the Brown Building where it stands today, where Iggy's grandmother died, two blocks from the apartment where Iggy's daughter lives.

In the years that followed, thousands more Americans died in growing violence from Iggy's government worldwide, far surpassing the death-toll of 1911, as well as surpassing the death-toll of 2001. Now, as then, there are no municipal fire trucks that reach that high, no helicopter rescue plans, and no one with BASE jump parachutes in Manhattan's skyscrapers.

Iggy's daughter Brooke plans to write a book. It will say the opposite of her late mother's lost manuscript.

33. DR. KARRY'S AMAZING DISCOVERY

It was a dark and stormy night. Thunder and lightning frightened Mazel, the little blonde dog, and she cowered against the leg of her owner, Dr. Roy Karry. He separated the fur on Mazel's neck and, with a pair of tweezers, gingerly picked out a flea, placed it in a tiny glass jar, and hurried downstairs to his laboratory, as the disheartened dog stared and whimpered.

Dr. Karry is the famous scientist who astounded the world with his many achievements, including his discovery years ago that time is not a separate entity; time is merely the perception of movement.

A mechanical clock is used for demonstrations whenever the concept is explained to any audience of the general public. "Clocks are mechanisms of regular movement by which other movement is measured," Dr. Karry would say when he began his presentations.

The discovery pointed toward the possibility of time travel.

If the entire universe were placed in a previously held position, with every atom having its previous state (direction, momentum, inertia, et cetera) then "time" would have been regressed, and the universe would continue onward again, repeating the same path.

Dr. Karry continued to perform research into the field of time travel in his hidden lab, safe from his adoring fans. In one of many experiments spanning years since his initial work, Dr. Karry placed a small flea in an observation chamber and recorded the insect's movements for one minute, while other equipment analyzed every aspect of the bug and its behavior down to the atomic level.

At the end of that minute of analysis, nanobots were released into the bug's chamber. Nanobots are microscopic robots that are able to move and rearrange single atoms. The nanobots were programmed to reassemble the flea in the exact condition and position it was one minute in the past, when the recording began.

Nanotechnology would ensure that the bug's atoms resumed the same state that each atom possessed one minute prior.

After its reassembly, the insect repeated exactly its movements from the previously recorded minute of activity.

The bots reassembled the flea again.

The reassembled bug repeated exactly its movements from the previously recorded minute of activity.

Dr. Karry cheered out loud in the empty lab as the experiment continued to be repeated over and over again. He hurried out of the room to issue a press release announcing his latest breakthrough.

Upon returning to the laboratory, Dr. Karry shut the door behind him and, following strict lab protocol, locked it. He walked across the room to the observation chamber and its ongoing experiment. The bug was not in the chamber. Dr. Karry asked himself aloud: "Where is the fl…"

Upon returning to the laboratory, Dr. Karry shut the door behind him and, following strict lab protocol, locked it. He walked across the room to the observation chamber and its ongoing experiment. The bug was not in the chamber. Dr. Karry asked himself aloud: "Where is the fl…"

Upon returning to the laboratory, Dr. Karry shut the door behind him and, following strict lab protocol, locked it. He walked across the room to the observation chamber and its ongoing experiment. The bug was not in the chamber. Dr. Karry asked himself aloud: "Where is the fl…"

Upon returning to the laboratory, Dr. Karry shut the door behind him and, following strict lab protocol, locked it. He walked across the room to the observation chamber and its ongoing experiment. The bug was not in the chamber. Dr. Karry asked himself aloud: "Where is the fl…"

[repeat ad infinitum]

(Postscript: This postscript is necessary because, of the many times that this classic story has been published or reprinted, sometimes a proofreader eliminates the final paragraph(s) in the mistaken belief that an error has occurred. That is not an error. That is the reason for some of the popular subtitles for this work, including: "The Longest Story Ever Written" and "The Never-Ending Story").

34. THE CRUCIFIX

I gave the naked guy in the seedy hotel a crucifix and he stopped crying. Sometimes a kind gesture is enough.

"Where'd you get the crucifix?" he murmured as he struggled to stand up from the hallway's floor.

"Why are you …uh… naked?" I stuttered, hoping he would forget his question about the crucifix's origin.

"Where Did You Get The Cross?" he demanded, using the wall to remain upright.

I backed up as I asked "Why were you crying?"

"WHERE DID YOU GET THIS SWASTIKA?!?!?" he screamed, echoing off all the doors of the floor.

My fist landed so hard that he hit the carpet.

I took the crucifix from the naked guy in the hotel as he started crying.

35. SHE WAS TEMPERAMENTAL

"Not yet," Avocado whispered to Bob; "Not yet. But soon!" she teased him. Bob's love for her was so large he could barely contain himself. So as the days passed, Bob tried not to pester Avocado. He knew that Avocado would warm up. it would just take a little time. One day soon Avocado would be ready, and oh what a glorious day that would be.

On Tuesday, Bob was in the bathroom, engaged in good personal hygiene, the details of which will not be elaborated here. Suddenly, Bob could hear Avocado scream... "I'M READY!" Bob could not believe his ears. Again Avocado's screaming came "HURRY! I'M READY ...NOW!" Bob hurried to drop what he was doing and pull up his pants. "EAT ME ... NOW!"

Bob jerked open the bathroom door and, clutching his undone belt, he sprinted down the hall toward the kitchen which was, now ...eerily ...silent. Bob was too late. As soon as he ran in, Bob could see that Avocado had changed. She looked sick. She had become quiet.

Avocado whispered sadly, "...too late. Too late. Toooo late."

It was over.

36. OLD SOVIET SOCIALIST POETRY

Poetry concerning the (former) Union of Soviet Socialist Republics -

There once was a land full of commies
who wanted government as a mommy
the bitch they got instead
is now diced up and dead
'cuz mommy made the commies all zombies

37. CAPITALIST PEARLS POETRY

Mixed economies are masochistic crimes
paying taxes to collectivist minds
stop feeding freedom's foes
it's self-defeating to throw
capitalist pearls before socialist swine

38. DEMOCRACY = DUMBOCRACY

Democracy is not poetry
It actually is a sin
vote and vote and vote again
'til libertarians give up
and socialists win

ABOUT THE AUTHOR

Supermodel (that's her on the cover) and superwriter Lin Xun bares all in this book about the USA's history. Lin, a history teacher, exposes her honey hole of American heritage, including these facts: (1) that the USA's Pledge of Allegiance was the origin of the Nazi salute and Nazi behavior; (2) Swastika's represented crossed "S" letter shapes for "socialist" under Hitler.

Lin is part of the Pointer Institute for Media Studies, as well as the avant garde Dead Writer's Club ("DWC" -an author's group).

Lin and the Pointer Institute provide remedial education to journalists about history, economics, government, and more. They un-tangle those twelve years of brainwashing that cripple news reporters.

The DWC also fights media incompetency and toward that goal it joined with the Pointer Institute in 2016 to shut down the Tampa Tribune Newspaper.

Lin's research skills (with the assistance of the author Micky Barnetti) resulted in the arrest, trial, conviction, and imprisonment of America's Dumbest Criminals (and the foreclosure of their homes, along with victim restitution liens, and criminal forfeiture judgments, in amounts totaling millions of dollars).

Micky Barnetti is a philologist and a forensic fraud analyst.

He is also a member of the Dead Writers Club.

Matt Crypto is an investigative journalist and researcher in the fields of anarchaeology and misanthropology.

Lin and the DWC are thankful for the ongoing support of No Pledge Publishing.

Other titles by the Dead Writers Club include: "Third Reich" http://www.amazon.com/dp/1517010268

"Drug Detection Dog Training – Libertarian Lawyers Fight Police State USA," at http://www.amazon.com/dp/1500735280

The self-titled "Dead Writers Club" is available at http://www.amazon.com/dp/150255898X

"BFFs Analects" is available at http://www.amazon.com/dp/1502368781

The groundbreaking book "Pledge of Allegiance & Swastika Secrets" (a semi-biographical work about the nation's leading authority on the Pledge of Allegiance and his many discoveries about its bizarre past and present) from No Pledge Publishing at http://www.amazon.com/dp/148121618X

The DWC also assisted with the following:

A classic science fiction tale revealing an amazing discovery about time travel at http://www.amazon.com/dp/1500588091

The book "World History" at http://www.amazon.com/dp/1511817488

"Lies My Teacher Told Me" is available at http://www.amazon.com/dp/1515248720

A biography of Francis Bellamy at http://www.amazon.com/dp/1515096874

"Liberal Fascism: The Secret history of American Nazism" at http://www.amazon.com/dp/1515314863

"Lies and the Lying Liars Who Tell Them" at http://www.amazon.com/dp/1515295931

"Mein Kampf by Adolf Hitler" at http://www.amazon.com/dp/1515356736

www.ingramcontent.com/pod-product-compliance
Lightning Source LLC
Chambersburg PA
CBHW060616290526
45793CB00001B/46